LONDON ON SEA

SARAH GUY

Illustrated by Emily Feaver

LONDON
ON SEA

50 CAPITAL DAYS OUT
ON THE COAST

SARAH GUY

EBURY
PRESS

CONTENTS

Entries run from East to West along the coast

Southwold 9

Walberswick 12

Dunwich 15

Thorpeness 17

Aldeburgh 19

Felixstowe 21

Harwich & Dovercourt 23

Walton-on-the-Naze 26

Frinton-on-Sea 30

Clacton-on-Sea 33

Southend-on-Sea 35

Leigh-on-Sea 38

Canvey Island 40

Whitstable 41

Herne Bay 44

Westgate-on-Sea 46

Margate 49

Broadstairs 51

Ramsgate 54

Deal 59

Dover 61

Folkestone 65

Sandgate 68

Hythe 71

Dungeness 73
Camber & Rye 77
Winchelsea Beach 80
Hastings 83
St Leonards-on-Sea 86
Bexhill 88
Pevensey Bay 92
Eastbourne 94
Seaford 99
Newhaven 100
Rottingdean 103
Brighton 105
Hove 109
Shoreham-by-Sea 111
Worthing 113
East Beach Littlehampton 116
West Beach Littlehampton & Climping 118
Bognor Regis 121
Selsey 125
East Wittering 127
West Wittering 129
Further Afield 133
Bournemouth 135
Hunstanton 138
Holkham 141
Sheringham 143
Cromer 146
Index 148

INTRODUCTION

Who doesn't love a day beside the sea? A chance to blow away the cobwebs, turn your face to the sun and breathe in the salty air; to hurtle down the helter-skelter or eat chips at the end of the pier; to go crabbing or shell-collecting; to walk along towering cliffs or through briny, bird-filled marshlands; and, most of all, to gaze at the endlessly fascinating and constantly changing sea.

Day tripping is such an established pastime that it's strange to think that the seaside jaunt only really took hold in the nineteenth century. Bathing cures kick-started the idea of a restorative holiday by the sea in the eighteenth century, fashionable types popularised the notion, and the arrival of the railways democratised it. Our idea of the quintessential resort includes a pier, a promenade, illuminations, ice-creams, crazy golf and amusement arcades, but the seaside archetype also encompasses everything from old smuggling villages to modern kitesurfing spots. Resorts change with the seasons, too, as beaches packed with sunbathers are reclaimed by solitary dog walkers and surfers in wetsuits.

Lucky Londoners have all kinds of coastal escapes within easy reach. As well as star beaches such as Camber and West Wittering, the choice includes traditional (Felixstowe, Herne Bay, Worthing), arty (Folkestone, Hastings, Margate), one-off (Leigh-on-Sea,

Dungeness, Thorpeness), chi-chi (Deal, Southwold, Whitstable) and urbane (Brighton, Bournemouth). Go for a special event (Broadstairs Folk Festival, Eastbourne Air Show), an architectural treat (De La Warr Pavilion, historic Harwich) or an unfamiliar landscape (Canvey Island, Dunwich). Whatever your preference, take a trip and make the most of the seaside on your doorstep.

SOUTHWOLD

Well-heeled Southwold is an Instagrammer's dream, with a cute pier, pastel beach huts, a working lighthouse and a picturesque ferry. South Green, a collection of gracious houses set around a green sward near the seafront, is a classic Southwold spot, but the whole town looks a treat, winter or summer.

The wooden pier is at the northern edge of the town, and along it are cafés, a small amusement arcade and Tim Hunkin's delightfully bonkers *Under the Pier Show*, a collection of automata and games. This end of Southwold is also home to a seasonal funfair, a nine-hole crazy-golf course and a model-yacht pond. The *Boating Lake Tearoom* offers good coffee and cake, plus more substantial snacks; children will want to feed the ducks.

The town centre is equally picture-perfect, and independent shops still outnumber the chains. Most shops and cafés are found on the High Street and Queen Street. Don't miss *Harris & James* – coffee roasters, and chocolate, cake and ice-cream makers. Flavours change, but they run from key lime pie to blackberry sorbet; even the wafers are own-made. The *Black Olive* deli's tempting stock includes Ginger Pig sausage rolls, while the *Two Magpies Bakery* has sourdough bread and baked doughnuts.

Adnams brewery is based in the town (tours are available), and many of the pubs and hotels are Adnams-owned – the *Crown* and the *Swan Hotel* are the big hitters.

The *Sailors' Reading Room* is a unique spot, filled with ships' figureheads, memorabilia and model ships – settle down with a newspaper and soak up the atmosphere. Make time to take in a film at the charming *Electric Picture Palace*, too.

Half a mile south of town, where the River Blythe separates Southwold from Walberswick, is Blackshore Quay. It's an easy walk – just head south along the Suffolk Coast Path, by the sand and shingle beach and alongside fields. The reward is a portion of *Mrs T's* fish and chips or a meal at the *Sole Bay Fish Company* (who also have a smokehouse and sell fresh fish). Further along, there's the *Harbour Café* and an Adnams pub, the *Harbour Inn*, plus a working boatyard. The views of black wooden huts and little jetties are a tonic, and there are plenty of crabbing spots. The foot ferry to Walberswick – a rowing boat – operates from here; the ferry company also runs trips along the River Blythe. If the water doesn't appeal, in summer there are horse-driven tours of Southwold on offer.

WALBERSWICK

Walberswick is lovely. A little too tasteful for some, perhaps, with each hollyhock just so and every cottage neater than the next. Crabbing from one of the many river inlets is about as exciting as it gets, but this slow pace suits visitors eager to escape the big city for a seaside idyll. The village is set back from the sea, separated by a line of dunes and black-painted beach huts (no jolly colours here). The unspoilt sand and shingle beach, reached by a boardwalk, is wonderfully moody in bad weather, and captivating when the sun shines. A little wooden hut near the River Blythe sells drinks and beach gear; in the smaller car park near the beach, an ice-cream van offers local ices and crabbing kits (buckets, bait and line). Otherwise, commerce is limited to a few shops, notably the *Parish Lantern* gift shop and tea room, which has a sheltered garden and serves Alder Tree Suffolk ice-cream. There are two decent pubs, the *Bell Inn* and the *Anchor*. The pretty village green has a children's play area.

There are lots of walks in and around Walberswick, with raised paths crossing any marshy patches: the South Coast Path runs along the beach from Dunwich; another long-distance footpath, the Sandlings Walk, cuts across the edge of the village.

Walberswick is divided from Southwold by the River Blythe; in summer, the rowing-boat ferry takes passengers across in a matter of minutes, so it's easy to pop across to Southwold's Blackshore Quay for quality fish and chips at *Mrs T's* and back again.

DUNWICH

Dunwich is a low-key but atmospheric pleasure, and a brilliant antidote to more chichi alternatives on the Suffolk coast. Birdwatchers will be in heaven. Spend the afternoon on the beach here, tucked behind the dunes, taking in the sweep of the coast from Walberswick to Sizewell. Apart from a swim or a trudge on the shingle, there's blissfully little to do. Fish and chips can be had at the *Flora Tearooms,* in the car park behind the beach. Dunwich village is barely a hamlet now, much reduced from its glory days in the thirteenth century, but it does have a pub (the *Ship*), the *Dingle Hill Tearooms* and a small museum, which documents the village's decline. On the edge of the village is the ruined *Greyfriars* friary.

South of Dunwich, Dunwich Heath is run by the National Trust, which operates a café near the car park. This, and a row of coastguard cottages, are pretty much the only buildings here. The shingle beach is backed by crumbling cliffs, on top of which is the glorious heath. There's wildlife galore, from adders and butterflies to birds and, in the woodland, deer; sometimes the heath is purple with heather, or bright with yellow gorse. Walk further south along the beach and you'll arrive at RSPB Minsmere: 2,400 acres of reed beds, heathland and woods, and home to scores of bird species.

THORPENESS

This picture-book village by the sea is its own little world, and quite unlike other resorts. It owes its existence to Glencairn Stuart Ogilvie, who built the village as a holiday playground in the early twentieth century. It's full of quirky buildings, most notably the *House in the Clouds* (built as a water tower), but there's also a windmill and plenty of idiosyncratic faux Tudor and Jacobean houses to marvel over (and stay in); the black-painted wooden cottages along Uplands Road are charming, too. One striking twenty-first-century addition is the *Dune House* on the beach, built by Living Architecture. The beach is mainly shingle, colonised in places by some impressive greenery – sea kale, campion, sea pea, sea spurge and even some rosehip bushes – but untouched by ice-cream kiosks. In winter it's fabulously bleak.

Thorpeness is very family-friendly – the picturesque boating lake, the Meare, is a highlight – and everything is within walking distance. the *Kitchen @ Thorpeness* is a great place to eat, for a full meal or a snack (the sausage rolls are made fresh every day). The only pub, the *Dolphin*, has a large beer garden; refreshments can also be had at the boating lake and at the golf club – the restaurant there is open to all and serves afternoon tea. Shops are limited to a village store behind the pub, a hut next to the Meare, and the *Thorpeness Emporium*, stuffed with bric-a-brac and a welcome diversion on inclement days. The great attraction of Thorpeness is that there are few attractions – for a bookshop or a cinema, head to Aldeburgh.

You can walk to Aldeburgh along the beach. There's a bus, too – supplemented in the summer holidays by the heritage buses operated by the Buckland Omnibus Company. In the other direction, you'll reach Sizewell Beach, where, as well as the monumental nuclear power station, there's an old-school café. The shingle beach here is peaceful, backed by dunes and dotted with plants; it's popular with dog walkers, as there are no seasonal restrictions.

ALDEBURGH

Forget sticks of rock and joke T-shirts, Aldeburgh is a posh, cultured seaside town that can sometimes feel a little smug. But the well-heeled gentility brings a raft of cafés (try *Munchies*) and restaurants, including a good fish and chip restaurant, the *Golden Galleon* (with a sister take-away, *Aldeburgh Fish & Chips,* along the street). Of the various pubs, the *White Hart* serves wood-fired pizza and Adnams ale. There's more than one wine merchant, lots of ice-cream options and several delis – the *Aldeburgh Market* deli and café has a wet fish stall and sells dressed crab. A few chains have infiltrated the high street, but independents dominate, notably the well-stocked *Aldeburgh Bookshop*. The town still has a fishing fleet, and the catch can be bought at huts near the promenade. An appealing cinema and a little summer theatre both add interest, and the boating pond on the seafront is a popular spot.

There are good walks, too, along the shingle beach towards Thorpeness (past Maggi Hambling's striking *Scallop* sculpture); in the other direction, just past a Landmark Trust-owned Martello tower, the seafront takes you as far as Slaughden Quay and the sailing club and no further. You can gaze at Orford Ness, a fascinating shingle spit managed by the National Trust, but to access it you need to travel by boat from Orford.

Aside from the seaside delights, the biggest draw is the Aldeburgh Festival in June (founded by one-time residents Benjamin Britten and Peter Pears), but visitors also come for the Literary Festival (March), the Food & Drink Festival (September), the Poetry Festival and the Documentary Film Festival (both November). The Aldeburgh Carnival, held over three days every August, is well-liked, too.

FELIXSTOWE

Felixstowe hasn't yet been rediscovered, which is what makes it so delightful. The glory days of this prime Edwardian resort are long gone, but there's still plenty to entertain day trippers. You can no longer arrive by paddle steamer from London, and the station has been reduced to one platform, but the legacy of the town's heyday includes some handsome buildings and the Seafront Gardens, restored and Grade II listed. These hug the cliff face behind the beach and, together with the low-key illuminations strung along the promenade, make for a classy seafront. There are amusements, a theatre (the *Spa Pavilion*) and a pier (restored in 2017). Families come for the miles of sand and shingle, lined with bright beach huts and the occasional kiosk. The all-day *Alex Brasserie* is a good spot for a bacon sandwich or a cocktail; there's a terrace overlooking the sea. Perched in the Gardens, *Chilli & Chives @ the Cliff Top* has a covetable location, too, and serves lunches and home-made cake.

For quieter beaches, head north towards Old Felixstowe; you can walk all the way along the front. Carry on past a couple of Martello towers and the golf course to reach the jetty, where a little foot ferry runs to Bawdsey. Around the jetty is a boatyard, a sailing club, a couple of cafés, a fresh-fish stall and the *Ferry Boat Inn*; on the Bawdsey side, there's

Bawdsey Radar, the world's first operational radar station and now a museum.

Heading south from the centre of town, on the Landguard Peninsula, there's a foot ferry that takes passengers to Harwich and Shotley. Also on this side of town is a nature reserve, the eighteenth-century *Landguard Fort* and *Felixstowe Museum*; you can walk here along the coast from Felixstowe town. Visible for miles is the Port of Felixstowe, Britain's busiest container port; you can get a close look from the designated viewing area near the fort.

The town centre is a little tired, but has enough independent shops to make browsing enjoyable. Most can be found on Hamilton Road and Orwell Road; don't leave without visiting *Poor Richard's*, a friendly second-hand and antiquarian bookshop.

HARWICH &
DOVERCOURT

Anyone with the slightest interest in nautical history
or evocative, old town centres should make a beeline
for Harwich. The *Mayflower* was (probably) built here
and Samuel Pepys was the MP. Evidence of the
centuries-old port and naval base is all around, from
the *Treadwheel Crane* to the *Redoubt Fort*; to see everything, follow the Maritime Heritage Trail. Look out
for charming details, too; even door knockers are fash-
ioned in the shape of fish or anchors. Shops and pubs
are concentrated on West and Church Streets. The
oldest house in Harwich, *Foresters* (built in 1450), is
on Church Street, as is the old Guildhall and tempting
antique shop the *Harwich Emporium* (confusingly, the
original sign reads 'Jackson'). Don't miss the elegant
facade of the 1911 *Electric Palace Cinema* on King's
Quay Street. Snug little pubs are everywhere – finding
a real ale is easy. Facing the water, the *Pier* (bar, restaurant and hotel) is the upmarket dining option, while
the shed-like *Café on the Pier* provides comfort food
if you don't fancy fish and chips. The truncated
Ha'penny Pier is an attraction in its own right, but
it's also where you catch the foot ferry to the Shotley
Peninsula, across the River Stour, and to Felixstowe.
Next to the pier is the bright-red *Lightvessel LV18*, a
decommissioned lighthouse ship.

A few steps further on, industrial Harwich stops abruptly and there's a sandy cove, complete with beach huts and a promenade. The shoreline is strewn with shells, pebbles and seaweed, and there are lots of sea birds: turnstones dart about and sanderlings swoop low. But look up, across the water, for a ringside view as huge cranes in the Port of Felixstowe unload mammoth container ships. Even the mighty ferries going to and from the Hook of Holland are dwarfed.

Along the prom is the *Low Lighthouse*, now used as a marine museum; beyond this, by Beacon Hill and World War II remnant the *Cornwallis Battery*, is a long stone breakwater where conflicting tides meet to scenic effect. Once you're around this corner, the full extent of Dovercourt Beach is apparent: acres of sand washed clean with every tide, adorned by two magnificent Victorian iron lighthouses. As the promenade continues, there are beach huts, watersports, cafés and lots of family-centred amusements, but really this is a beach made for sandcastle-building and shell-collecting. Dovercourt's shops and cafés can be found in and around Main Road – just look for the imposing statue of Queen Victoria and head inland.

To extend the walk, continue on the coastal path into marshland and mudflats, or take the Essex Way long-distance path into the countryside to Wrabness and Manningtree.

WALTON-ON-THE-NAZE

Visiting Walton-on-the-Naze is a bit like stepping back in time, with old-school pleasures such as dodgems, sandcastles and kites to the fore, and a nice cup of tea as the drink of choice. Just steps from the shore, the centre of town has seen better days, but it is worth a small detour for fish and chips at *Yates* or a pint at the *Victory*; Old Pier Street and the High Street are where the shops and caffs are concentrated. But there's so much more to Walton: as well as the family-friendly beach, there are fascinating bits of history, nature and geology to uncover.

Stretching out to sea is one of the longest pleasure piers in the UK; it's a hulking structure, housing an array of slot machines, a tenpin bowling alley and a popular amusement park with lots of children's rides – come here to brave the ghost train or twirl around in a tea cup. Either side of the pier are miles of golden sands, divided by seaweed-coated groynes and backed by stacked rows of prettily painted beach huts. The beach – which almost disappears at high tide – is speckled with shells; you might also find a fossil. The walk south leads to Frinton-on-Sea, but head north, either on the beach or along the top, to reach the Naze. Once there, stand on the Crag Walk sea defence for the best view of the red cliffs, populated by swooping sand martins and fast eroding.

The Naze is Walton's USP, a grassy headland surrounded by water on three sides, patterned by nature trails and home to the *Naze Tower* (built in 1720 as a navigational aid). The views from the tower are worth the climb up the spiral staircase: you can see the cranes at Harwich port, huge wind turbines out at sea and sailing boats in Titchmarsh Marina. The tower doubles as an art gallery and a tea room, with home-made cakes and snacks. There are World War II relics on the peninsula, too – including pill boxes that have slipped from the cliff on to the beach. Beyond the Naze is Hamford Water National Nature Reserve, made up of creeks, salt marshes and mud- and sand-flats, home to seals and important for wildfowl. It's possible to explore this beguiling area on a boat trip (from the marina) in the summer.

Walton-on-the-Naze

FRINTON-ON-SEA

Straight-laced Frinton is nothing like its near neighbour, Clacton, and even manages to make Walton-on-the-Naze appear raffish, though the resort has loosened up a bit since it was developed in the late nineteenth century. It was designed to keep out the riffraff (no pier, no pub), and the posh hotels and houses attracted the likes of Winston Churchill and Ivor Novello. These days it has a pub, the *Lock & Barrel*; an ice-cream parlour, *Pop-Pins*; and several fish and chip shops – try *Young's Other Plaice*. However, it doesn't have, or need, amusement arcades, bowling alleys or funfairs. Entertainment comes in the form of Frinton Summer Theatre (a different play every week in high season) and in sports (there are tennis, cricket and golf clubs). Connaught Avenue is the main drag, an engaging street close to the beach with a choice of cafés. Independent shops include a fine fishmonger's, *Young's*; a welcoming Scandi shop, *Great Danes*; and a lovely bookshop, *Caxton Books*.

It's a great place to re-enact a certain sort of bucket-and-spade childhood. The seafront is a delight, with well-kept shelters, a little clock tower and a thatched toilet block. The Greensward runs parallel to the promenade and is a handy spot for picnics and Frisbee-throwing. The cliff drops down to a sandy beach partitioned by gnarled groynes and washed clean by the tide. There are colourful beach huts, including some on stilts that hang over the water at high tide. The only reminder of the modern world is the giant wind farm on the horizon.

Frinton's architecture is also captivating, from the grand dwellings on The Esplanade and 'the Avenues' (First Avenue, Second Avenue, and so on), to the Art Deco beauties to the east of town (look in and around Central Avenue, Cliff Way and Graces Walk). These 1930s houses are all that exists of the planned Frinton Park Estate: Oliver Hill (architect of the Midland Hotel, Morecombe) was commissioned to design 1,000 Art Deco houses, and while the project was begun in 1934, it was abandoned two years later. The thatched tennis club on Holland Road is worth a look, too.

Head eastwards along the coast and you're soon in Walton-on-the-Naze – at low tide you can walk on the beach; for a longer stroll (about five miles), go west on the sea wall, past Holland-on-Sea, to Clacton.

CLACTON-ON-SEA

Trippers originally came to Clacton-on-Sea by steam-ship, from London to Clacton Pier; all that survives of that tradition is the occasional excursion on the paddle steamer *Waverley*, but the pier is still going strong. Opened in 1871, these days it holds a circus, a funfair, amusement arcades, tenpin bowling and the *Seaquarium*; you can even get your fortune told. If that sounds like too much excitement, just walk to the end of the pier and gaze out to sea at the Gunfleet Sands Offshore Wind Farm. The sandy beach stretches out for miles on either side of the pier, and although Clacton can get busy, it's easy to find a spot to set up camp. Near the pier, the promenade has ice-cream and refreshment stops. It's a short walk west past beach huts and a Martello tower to a children's playground; go eastwards to Holland-on-Sea for quieter beaches and classy snack kiosk The *Beach Haven*.

Clacton's attractions are traditional; it doesn't do fancy, but it does do fun. The beach is made for bucket-and-spade activities and the vibrant seafront gardens are a tribute to the council gardeners. Food and drink options are equally old-school, right down to the *Tubby Isaacs* seafood stall near the entrance to the pier. Stalwart caffs serving eggs on toast and cups of tea abound: at the *Coffee Bean Café*, leaf tea is served in china cups, while the headline dish at the *Kabin Café* is pie, mash and liquor. Fish and chips are easy to find, too. The tidy town centre is close to the beach and worth a wander. Take home smoked fish from *Ken Green Fish Merchants* or craft supplies from the *Wool Cabin*, or just poke around the many charity shops.

For further diversions, come in August for the Air Show (just before the bank-holiday weekend) and for the week-long carnival.

SOUTHEND-ON-SEA

For many years the East Enders' resort of choice, Southend is now a mix of good-time holiday destination and busy commuter town. The high street is bustling but anodyne; the party only starts at the seafront. It's easy to find a spot on the sand and shingle beach – it stretches for miles – but the Three Shells Beach near the pier is popular with families as it has a safe bathing lagoon. Clustered nearby are amusement arcades, casinos, pubs, cafés and restaurants – *Bailey's Fry Inn* is the top choice for fish and chips. There's a tenpin bowling alley in the Grade II listed *Kursaal*. Either side of the pier is the *Adventure Island* fun park, which looks exactly as a funfair should, with a brightly coloured helter-skelter and a twisting rollercoaster. Southend Pier is Grade II listed, and it is the longest pleasure pier in the world, extending for well over a mile into the sea – it's a curious sensation to be so far from land without being on a boat. Whether you walk or take the train, you have to pay, and dogs aren't allowed. There's an RNLI lifeboat station and a modern pavilion with a no-frills café at the far end, but the views are the main attraction: giant ships sail along the Thames Estuary, and the Isles of Grain and Sheppey and the north Kent coast appear within reach. This is also the docking point for the paddle steamer *Waverley*, which runs from here to Whitstable and to Tower Bridge in London.

The Cliff Gardens rise up behind the seafront and provide landscaped green space all the way to Westcliff;

at the top of the cliffs is Royal Terrace, a pretty row of Georgian villas, and the *Royal Hotel*. Built in 1791, and no longer a hotel but now a cocktail bar and restaurant, it's a good spot for afternoon tea or cocktails. The 1912 funicular, the Cliff Lift, is closed indefinitely, but there's also a modern lift between the seafront and the town.

East along the front, past the *Sea Life Adventure* aquarium, are the upmarket environs of Thorpe Bay. Beach huts and sailing boats replace the bright lights and slot machines, and the beaches are less busy. The *Roslin Beach Hotel's* sun terrace is a good spot for a coffee or a slap-up meal.

In the other direction, it's a lovely walk along the prom to Westcliff, past waterside cafés such as *Oliver's on the Beach* and the *Beach Hut*. Although Westcliff merges seamlessly into Southend-on-Sea, it's very much its own place. The main shopping street, Hamlet Court Road, was a smart affair in the early twentieth century, and although that's no longer true, a little of the gentility remains. Come to Westcliff for a more mellow experience (no funfair here), the 1960s Cliffs Pavilion (which gets touring West End shows) and a good choice of places to eat. It's hard to beat The Arches – a row of cafés and fish and chip restaurants built into the cliff face, overlooking the seafront. *Rossi's* ice-cream parlour, on the Esplanade, is another well-known landmark.

Carry on to Chalkwell, home to the annual Village Green arts festival (held in lovely Chalkwell Park) and an even less crowded beach; further still is Leigh-on-Sea. You can also cycle the route – there's a bike path that runs all the way along the coast.

LEIGH-ON-SEA

What Leigh-on-Sea lacks in beach it more than makes up for in cockle sheds, pubs and expansive estuary views. The fishing village of Old Leigh – divided from the rest of Leigh by the railway line – is an atmospheric spot, with cobbles, ancient drinking haunts (check out the *Crooked Billet*) and seafood sheds. Buy a tub of prawns and watch the boats go by – Leigh has an active fishing fleet and the water's edge is lined with boatyards and wharves; equally fascinating are the container ships going to and from the Port of Tilbury, further up the Thames Estuary. (Fish fresh off the boats can be bought at *Osborne & Sons* fishmongers and *Leigh Fisherman's Co-op*.) If you'd rather not eat on the hoof, head to the *Mayflower* pub for fish and chips, to *Sara's Tea Garden*, or to the *Boatyard*, a well-regarded restaurant with big windows overlooking the water. Like the pubs in Old Leigh, this is a good venue in the evening, too.

When the tide's out, there's a small stretch of sand for bucket-and-spade activities; beyond the sand, glistening mudflats dotted with beached sailing boats are revealed. The seafront path goes all the way along the coast to Thorpe Bay in the east; in the other direction, you can walk to Benfleet, a flat four-mile stroll that takes you past Two Tree Island nature reserve, Hadleigh Castle Country Park and along the Thames Estuary.

For a wider choice of cafés and restaurants, cross the railway line and walk up the hill to the more modern part of Leigh. Leigh Broadway is an engaging high street, and it's easy to spend a couple of hours poking around the shops and refuelling at cafés such as *Birdwood*, *Stop the World* or *Milly's* (the last is slightly further on in Leigh Road, but with the bonus of a garden at the back).

To see the town in full swing, come for the annual Leigh Folk Festival, held over several days in June.

CANVEY ISLAND

More visually rewarding in winter than in summer, Canvey Island is an intriguing place. Off-season, you can enjoy walking through a pleasingly melancholy mix of empty beach, mudflats, open spaces, marshland and industrial detritus, with views changing from amusement park and brightly painted blue sea wall to oil terminals and a busy shipping lane. Giant container and cruise ships sail up and down the Thames, heading to and from the Port of Tilbury and passing very close to Canvey Island. The Isle of Grain looks almost near enough to swim to across the Thames Estuary. There's a whole host of birds to spot, too. Spend a day here and really see the island – follow the sea wall and just keep going.

In any season, you can take in the view from the comfort of The *Labworth*, a restored 1930s building on the seafront between the Western and Eastern Esplanades. The café here serves slap-up breakfasts (including a vegetarian option) and every table has a great view; the restaurant is equally popular – book ahead, especially for the Christmas lunches (served from the end of November). In summer, nearby Thorney Bay beach is a child-friendly spot, with picnic tables, a playground and plenty of sand.

WHITSTABLE

Once upon a time, oysters were Whitstable's main attraction, but now people come for the shops and restaurants – some of which serve the famous bivalves. The Whitstable vibe is an appealing mix of working harbour and metropolitan chic: incomers have changed the nature of what was once a fishing town, but the atmosphere hasn't entirely disappeared and the new money keeps the butcher's, baker's and greengrocer's afloat alongside the gift shops and boutiques. High Street and Harbour Street form the centre of town; independents rule here and you can easily spend a happy afternoon browsing the boutiques, bookshops, record stores, second-hand shops and delis. Visitors from East London will recognise the *Eat 17* convenience store. It's also worth exploring the little lanes and alleys that run between the town and the shore, which make the centre of town so winsome.

Quality cafés and restaurants are too many to mention, and options range from top-notch coffee at *Blueprint Coffee*, via doorstop sandwiches at *Windy Corner Stores,* to bistro fare at *Samphire. Wheelers Oyster Bar* is an institution. Whitstable isn't short of pubs, either, and many of them have music in the evenings; The *Twelve Taps* specialises in craft beer. The knockout local restaurant is The *Sportsman*, just along the coast in Seasalter – book well in advance for this one.

There's so much to see and do in town that the beach can get forgotten. Out to sea are the Kentish Flats Offshore Wind Farm and the Maunsell Forts, relics from World War II. The beach itself is less exciting – a strip of shingle, divided by wooden groynes, home to a few boats and backed by quirky dwellings – but it is nonetheless a pleasant spot in which to sink a pint from the *Old Neptune*, sample seafood from The *Forge* hut or wolf down fish and chips from *VC Jones*. Just along from the Neptune is the *Royal Native Oyster Stores* restaurant, and a little further east is the harbour, packed with many more eating options. Here, amid the black-painted fishermen's huts, the quays and slipways, and the industrial fixtures and fittings, there's a fishmarket, food stalls and unpretentious restaurants such as the *Crab & Winkle*. Just up the hill from the harbour is Whitstable Castle (more like a big house and garden than a true castle), where the *Orangery* serves teas. Beyond the harbour, it's an easy walk to Tankerton, past the Hotel Continental, brightly painted beach huts and green slopes; the rewards are an emptier beach, and a snack at local favourite *JoJo's*. Cyclists can arrive in Whitstable on the Crab & Winkle Way, a disused railway line running from Canterbury.

In summer, come prepared for crowds and book ahead for any restaurant you have your heart set on. It's even livelier during the Oyster Festival (July) and the Whitstable Biennale (every other June).

HERNE BAY

Delightfully unreconstructed Herne Bay couldn't be more different than its near neighbour Whitstable. Herne Bay was established as a seaside destination in the 1830s and was once quite the resort, vigorously promoted for its healthy air and hours of sunshine. These days, it's a quiet but appealing town – catch it before it changes.

All the elements for a good day by the sea are here: a pier, a little harbour, a clock tower, smart promenade gardens, amusement arcades, beach huts, ice-cream parlours and fish and chip shops. Every pub seems to be tied to Shepherd Neame. The beach is partitioned by wooden groynes and is a mix of shingle and, once the tide goes out a bit, sand. Along the Western Esplanade and Central Parade there are fish restaurants and cafés, many with tables outside overlooking the sea; *Le Petit Poisson* is a popular spot. The short pier is lined with beach huts housing shops and cafés serving everything from pizza to champagne and oysters; at the end is a small funfair with a merry-go-round and a helter-skelter. Out to sea are the remains of a much longer pier. More sea views can be had from Neptune's Arm, the short harbour wall. Back on the prom, there's a huge enclosed bandstand, complete with a branch of *Makcari's* café and ice-cream parlour.

Parallel to the beach is Mortimer Street, a pleasant, partially pedestrianised shopping street. Just off it, on William Street, is the *Seaside Museum*, which houses some interesting bits and pieces, including posters from Herne Bay's glory days. Further inland is the High Street – it's not particularly attractive, but it is home to the 1940s-styled *Vintage Empire* tea room, plus several antique arcades and junk shops where the prices are notably lower than in Margate or Whitstable. The *Emporium* and *Briggsy's* are good for a rummage.

Strike out west along the trim front and you come to Hampton Pier, a stubby concrete walkway with good views out to sea, or walk east along the promenade on the Oyster Bay Trail towards the ruins of *Reculver Towers*, three miles away. In either direction, it's hard to ignore the wind farm on the horizon.

WESTGATE-ON-SEA

Westgate's architectural legacy gives the place a very different look to other local resorts. Conceived in the 1860s as an exclusive holiday resort – Westgate-on-Sea Estate – the town retains many handsome Victorian and Edwardian buildings. The main drag, Station Street, is given charm by the canopied shops and the splendid *Carlton Cinema*, a Swiss-Gothic construction that originally served as the town hall. Visit the *Heritage Centre* (in St Saviour's Church, itself part of the original estate) for more information. Westgate was also the site of the first bungalow in England, built by John Taylor; he built more in nearby Birchington-on-Sea, where one Grade II listed example survives.

Station Street is where most of the shops and cafés can be found: one-offs such as a grocer's and a small garden centre mix with charity and bric-a-brac shops; *Westgate Fish 'n' Chips* is a popular take-away, while the *Bake & Alehouse* microbrewery and *Frederick's* tea room are handy for the cinema.

Standing on the grass-topped cliffs, it's obvious why developers chose the site. The two bays, St Mildred's and West Bay, have great stretches of sand, equally good for long walks with a dog in winter or playing beach games in summer. St Mildred's beach is marked by concrete groynes, and the sand gives way to exposed chalk peppered with rock pools at high tide. A few beach huts cluster near the food concessions; *Millie's Bar* stays open in the evenings. There's a choice of promenade or cliff walks; the clifftop has winding, sunken paths, hidden by hedges and ideal for blustery days. Walk east from here and you're soon in Margate. In the other direction, *Reculver Towers* can be seen in the far distance; before that, the huge sweep of sand is West Bay. Here there are more beach chalets and the *West Bay Café* (their proud boast, 'open 363 days a year', is a welcome sight in winter months). Keep walking west, through Birchington-on-Sea, and you'll reach Minnis Bay, with more lovely views and a restaurant/bar.

MARGATE

There's a lot of fun to be had in Margate, summer or winter. These days, the town has an arty, metropolitan vibe that means Londoners don't have to leave their big-city fixes behind. Whether it's fancy grilled cheese at *Cheesy Tiger*, Scandi-influenced snacks and coffee at *Mala Kaffe* (both out on the Harbour Arm), inventive pizza at the *Great British Pizza Company* (on the seafront), or superior seafood at *Hantverk & Found* (in the Old Town), good food isn't hard to find. There are masses of drinking haunts in and around the Old Town; many of the bars and brasseries on Marine Drive have great views, as does the Harbour Arm.

The *Turner Contemporary* gallery only opened in 2011, but it has bedded in fast; go for the art, but also to take in the view from its prime position on the seafront. *Dreamland*, the historic funfair reopened in 2015, is a retro treat, not only for rides such as the 1940s waltzer but also for old-time arcade games and the roller disco. Fans of the past will enjoy rummaging in the second-hand and antique shops in and around Market Street, King Street and Fort Road. There are also gift shops and galleries galore. All this fancy new stuff sits alongside old-school candy floss, fish and chip shops and amusement arcades. The well-preserved *Tudor House* and the kitsch *Shell Grotto* are worth a visit, too.

You don't have to spend money here to have a good time: Margate Main Sands is a big sweep of beach that's home to beach volleyball, picnics and sandcastles in the warmer months, but also a lovely place to walk in winter and a perfect location in any season for watching the sun set (inspiration for one JMW Turner). And if this beach gets too crowded, there's more golden sand just around the corner. Walk just west for Westbrook Bay, or go east along the prom, past the Turner Contemporary and the *Winter Gardens* theatre, towards the suburb of Cliftonville and Walpole Bay. In Cliftonville, afternoon tea is served at the quirky *Walpole Bay Hotel* and at local institution *Batchelor's Patisserie*. Check out *Haeckels* (Margate-made skincare) and *Simply Danish* (collectable furniture and homewares) on the way. Walk further in the same direction on the clifftop Viking Coastal Trail, and in around two miles you'll reach dramatic Botany Bay, then, in five miles, Broadstairs.

BROADSTAIRS

Broadstairs has an old-fashioned air, right down to its pretty clifftop bandstand, though more than one modish shop has started to appear among the family-run greengrocers and candy-floss merchants. The clifftop setting adds to its charm, and the sandy beaches are a treat, summer or winter. References to Charles Dickens, a frequent visitor to the town, are everywhere, and there's a Dickens Festival held every summer. Lurid tales of smuggling are also a running theme.

There's plenty of beach to go round, and it's easy to walk between many of them (though watch out for the tide). The beaches are sandy, though chalk reef is exposed at low tide. Viking Bay is the main town beach, a sweep of sand backed by cliffs and beach huts; St Mary's Bay and Stone Bay are the next two beaches heading north and are generally quieter than Viking Bay. A couple of miles north is popular surfing beach Joss Bay; north of that is Botany Bay, known for its dramatic chalk stacks. Less busy (and dog-friendly all year round) is Dumpton Gap, on the outskirts heading towards Ramsgate. All the beaches can be reached by walking or cycling the Viking Coastal Trail.

Broadstairs Folk Week transforms the town every August, with over 70 events (gigs, dances and work-shops) each day. There's music in the town the rest of the year, too, with many of the pubs featuring live music: have a pint in The *Chapel*, where real ale is served in a quirky old building filled with hundreds of second-hand books. If music doesn't do it for you, check out the *Palace Cinema*, a little independent gem with just 111 seats.

Shopping activity is mainly based around the High Street, York Street and Albion Street. Typical of the new breed of shops is *Kit*, a lifestyle store (clothes, homewares, gifts) that wouldn't look out of place in Shoreditch. Equally metropolitan is *Wyatt & Jones*, which serves knockout modern British food in a brasserie setting close to the beach. Word is out, so book ahead for dinner. *Bessie's Tea Parlour* is where to go if you're after home-made cakes, vintage cake stands and a wide range of teas. *Morelli's* gelateria has been in the same premises since 1932, and is much-photographed; the choice runs from a single scoop to an OTT sundae.

RAMSGATE

For visual drama on a seaside excursion, come to Ramsgate. There's almost too much to process in one day, what with the harbour, the marina, the cliffs, the tunnels and the grand architectural reminders of what a big-hitter the town once was, both as a resort and as a strategic base.

The place is dotted with blue plaques, a testament to its pulling power in the nineteenth century: Queen Victoria, Samuel Taylor Coleridge and Wilkie Collins are just a few of the notables who spent time here. Architect Augustus Pugin designed and lived in The *Grange* (now owned by the Landmark Trust but open for tours on Wednesdays), and there's the Pugin Town Trail, which takes you past buildings designed by members of the Pugin family. Aside from their brand of Gothic Revival, there are some glorious Georgian and Victorian streets and squares to be explored (Liverpool Lawn, for example); a walk along the clifftop promenade will give you a taster, but venture inland for the bigger picture.

The town centre is bigger than it first appears, with plenty of independent shops and old-fashioned cafés in and around High Street, King Street and Queen Street; for fish and chips, head to *Sunrise*. *Petticoat Lane Emporium*, in an old warehouse on Dumpton Park

Drive, is a little further, but worth the stroll if you're fond of second-hand rummaging.

For a more modern vibe, head to Addington Street, where *Vinyl Head* offers good coffee and global snacks while a turntable spins, or to *26 Harbour Street* for craft beer and live music. *Albion House* boutique hotel has a modern bar and restaurant, too – *Townleys*.

From the centre of town, it's a steep drop down to the Royal Harbour (a title bestowed by George IV, making it the only royal harbour in the country); find out more in the *Maritime Museum*, housed in the handsome Clock House on the harbour. Visit in July during regatta week to see it at its most hectic, or in December to see the boats rigged out with festive lights for the Ramsgate Illuminations. The marina, protected by the harbour, is packed with vessels; behind is a magnificent set of arches, occupied by marine businesses, shops and cafés. Check out *Archive* (a Scandinavian café and homestore) and *Arch 16* (jumble and vintage). The simple one-room *Sailor's Church* at the edge of the harbour is worth a look, too.

Ramsgate Main Sands beach is beyond the harbour, below East Cliff, and is perfect for making sandcastles. Looming over the beach are a Grade II listed pavilion (now restored by the Wetherspoon chain) and the cliffs, into which are built over three miles of tunnels. Used as an air-raid shelter during World War II, the *Ramsgate Tunnels* are open for tours. Continue along the top of East Cliff and, in a couple of miles, you'll reach Broadstairs – before you set off, pop into *Sorbetto* for a sugar boost. Attractions on this side of town include the *King George VI Memorial Park* and the *Italianate Glasshouse*. Over on the other side of the harbour, the stately West Cliff promenade leads to great views of Pegwell Bay, and another generous stretch of sand.

DEAL

Deal is the perfect destination for a grown-up, stress-free break: charming, easily accessible by train and with a fine selection of pubs. The compact town centre resembles a film set, with rows of Georgian houses and fishermen's cottages leading to a shingle beach lined with boats. No wonder legions of Londoners have snapped up sea-view properties, and the DFL (Down From London) influence can be seen in the growing number of upmarket shops and restaurants.

There's little that's garish here – even the amusement arcade is low-key, and the must-visit fish and chip shop, *Middle Street Fish Bar,* is tucked away on one of Deal's prettiest streets. The pier is similarly unshowy, with nothing on it except fishermen and a no-nonsense café at the end. Sit here over a fry-up and watch the waves and the changing weather through the huge glass windows. You can see the French coast and the ferries crossing to and from Dover.

The thriving High Street, and the little streets leading off it, are perfect for mooching, with a mix of charity shops and shabby-chic vintage stores such as *Mileage*. Intrepid independents include *Smugglers Records*: as well as selling CDs and vinyl, Smugglers also organises gigs and runs a record label. Also appealing are the *Hoxton Store* (carefully curated homewares from a proprietor who once had a shop in east London) and *Le Pinardier* wine shop and bar. The *Bakehouse* is just one of many excellent food outlets – it's only open until the scrumptious cakes and pastries run out, so get there in the morning. There's an interesting Saturday market (bric-a-brac, flowers and food, mostly), too – some of the dealers sell stuff they've brought over from France.

When it comes to restaurants, top pick is *Frog & Scot*, a friendly bistro serving stellar food, or the fancier *Victuals & Co*. For something a little more casual, try the *Black Douglas*, a boho café serving good coffee, hot snacks and big breakfasts – it's a great place to sit and read the papers. You're spoilt for choice when it comes to drinking haunts, from the *Hoy* (for wood-fired pizza) to the trad vibe of The *Ship*, but it's hard to resist the siren call of The *Bohemian*. Close to the seafront, this is a laid-back, late-opening pub with a tucked-away beer garden and generous plates of food.

Deal runs seamlessly into Walmer; both have castles, though Walmer's is rather grander than Deal's, with lovely gardens and an ace tea room (check out the sausage rolls). It's an easy, scenic stroll along the Saxon Shore Way, with the shingle beach, dotted with wild fennel and sea kale, only yards away. Walk as far as Kingsdown and the reward is a pint on the beach outside the *Zetland Arms*.

DOVER

If you like history, Dover is the day trip of dreams. From mighty Dover Castle to World War II remnants, you can't move in this town without being reminded of its glorious past. As the closest English port to mainland France, its strategic importance was immense. Its present is a little more lacklustre, with a workaday town centre dominated by the A20, though the Western Docks Revival regeneration project is underway (promising shops, restaurants and a new marina, as well as a cargo terminal), as is the redevelopment of the St James area of central Dover.

The seafront enclave around Waterloo Crescent, with streets of stately Victorian terraces, gives a glimpse of what an elegant place it once was, before World War II bombardment and post-war town planning. The beach is shingle and well-kept; there are refreshment kiosks and a swimming zone, and some modern landscaping. But, really, you're here to watch ships go by. On one side is the harbour (and a marina), with boats coming and going, and on the other is the ferry terminal, with ships heading to and from Calais and Dunkirk. Smaller boats can be booked for trips to see seals, the White Cliffs and the Goodwin Sands, site of many shipwrecks.

The castle – well-preserved and run by English Heritage – can occupy the best part of a day, and the views from it are far-reaching. It sits on a hill to the east of the town; on the opposite hill is Western Heights, now a nature reserve, but dotted with disused fortifications.

The Saxon Shore Way takes you on a scenic clifftop walk out of Dover, along the famous White Cliffs, past *South Foreland Lighthouse* to the shingle beach and *Coastguard* pub at St Margaret's Bay (and beyond to Walmer and Deal). There are cafés along the way.

WEATHER IS A THIRD TO PLACE AND TIME

FOLKESTONE

Folkestone vies with Margate for the title of artiest place on the Kent coast. There's no point in taking sides, just enjoy the fact that both towns offer a great day out for the arts-inclined visitor. While Margate has the Turner Contemporary gallery, Folkestone has the Triennial arts festival, which has bestowed a growing number of permanent artworks around the town since it was established in 2008. You can happen across the sculptures, plaques, monuments and sound installations, or tick them all off by following the Folkestone Artworks map.

There's plenty more to Folkestone than art, though – it has everything a day tripper needs for a seaside excursion. Though the town was badly bombed in World War II, many handsome Victorian and Edwardian buildings remain as a reminder of the town's heyday (though it's a shame that the Leas Lift, the water-operated funicular, has been mothballed). The adjacent *Grand* and The *Metropole* hotel buildings are particularly splendid. There are lots of well-kept parks and gardens, too – pretty Kingsnorth Gardens, near Folkestone Central Station, is a fine example.

A massive regeneration project aims to give the town a second golden era, and a great swathe of the seafront and beach is being remodelled over several years. Projects include the restoration of the Harbour

Arm (the terminus for the long-vanished boat train) – it's colonised at the weekends by food trucks and café-bars. Walk out on it any day of the week for the art and the unbeatable views from the end of the Arm: out to sea, or back to town and the chalk cliffs. The railway viaduct across the harbour is being transformed into a pedestrian walkway, and a beautiful winding boardwalk made of reclaimed railway sleepers now snakes across Shingle Beach, linking it to the Lower Leas Coastal Park.

The town centre lies between Folkestone Central Station and the sea; the most interesting area is the Creative Quarter, based around the Old High Street, Tontine Street and Rendezvous Street. The *Silver Screen Cinema* and the *Quarterhouse* arts centre are here, together with a cluster of independent cafés, bars and shops. One of the best cafés is *Steep Street*, a coffee and wine bar with a sideline in second-hand books; also worth a look are *Googies* and *Eleto Chocolate Café*, both of which have outdoor tables. *Big Boys Burger Co* and *Beano's* (vegetarian) are further options; for fish and chips, venture a few streets away to *Papa's*. The warren of streets lends itself to browsing: there are galleries, vintage shops and record stores, plus classy gift shops such as the *Great British Shop* and delightful one-offs such as *Rennies* (twentieth-century art and objects).

The seafront is one of the loveliest – and most interesting – on the south coast (though the gargantuan *Grand Burstin Hotel* on the edge of the harbour is hard to ignore). To the east of Folkestone Harbour,

Sunny Sands is a big crescent of sand popular with families and overlooked by Cornelia Parker's *The Folkestone Mermaid*; beyond is the Warren Beach and country park, a favourite spot for longer walks. Fish and seafood stalls dot the edge of the harbour, and there are several options for fish and chips; it's also the location of Folkestone's smartest restaurant, *Rocksalt*.

But head west for the jewel in Folkestone's crown, the linear Lower Leas Coastal Park, which runs parallel to Shingle Beach and Mermaid Beach (both pebbly). This charming park has three elements: a formal section, with impressive gardens; a wild area; and a 'fun zone', with a large, free adventure playground. There are lots of paths up and down the park – including the zigzag path – so you can easily drop down from the top of the cliffs (home to various works of art and an exquisite Art Nouveau bandstand) to the beachside promenade. There's enough space at this end of town to get away from any crowds; for a longer stroll, the prom will take you all the way to Sandgate.

SANDGATE

A classy little resort just along the coast from Folkestone, Sandgate is known for its antique shops and its HG Wells connection. Happily for the day tripper, it also has above-average food and drink options and a quiet beach.

The pebble beach is backed by a promenade – it's an easy one-mile stroll to the bright lights of Folkestone in one direction, and an equally flat three-mile walk to the slightly dimmer lights of Hythe in the other. The Royal Military Canal starts on the Hythe side of town; the path beside it runs for 28 tranquil miles to near Hastings. The six Martello towers in the hills and tiny *Sandgate Castle* on the seafront are further indicators of the town's past as a defensive hub.

Apart from the high street, which runs parallel to the seafront, and the little lanes near the beach, there's not much to interest the day tripper, but the leafy backstreets rising up the hill make a pleasant backdrop. Besides antique and junk shops, the main drag is lined with restaurants and coffee shops, and gift shops such as the *Sandgate Trading Company*. There's a good choice of pubs, including the *Inn Doors Micropub*. Eateries punch above their weight: *Roka* offers top-notch pizza; *Orchard Lane Coffee House* is a metropolitan-style coffee stop; *Comemos* is a deli-café with Spanish leanings; and the *Boat House* café is the place for a bacon roll beside the sea. The essence of Sandgate – seemingly casual but actually well-presented and carefully executed – is best captured by *Loaf.* This dog-friendly café has mismatched furniture and a low-key vibe, but the waiting staff are mustard-keen and the quality of the cakes, snacks and coffee is high.

Come during the August Bank Holiday weekend for the Sandgate Sea & Food Festival, when food stalls and live music take over the promenade, and there's a firework display.

HYTHE

Quiet, unassuming Hythe is full of surprises. *St Leonard's Ossuary*, containing more than a thousand skulls, is the most disconcerting, whereas the *tin chapel* (now the Tin Tabernacle arts centre), is simply a visual treat. And who doesn't want to ride on the Romney, Hythe & Dymchurch Railway? (It goes all the way to Dungeness.) The layout of Hythe is out of the ordinary, too – the town is bisected by the Royal Military Canal, a sleepy waterway that makes for a great town-centre or long-distance (28-mile) walk.

The high street is one side of the canal, the beach is on the other. The prom is level with the shingle and the beach isn't very wide, so you feel blissfully close to the water even when walking on concrete. The promenade runs in a straight line all the way from Sandgate until it comes to an abrupt end at Fisherman's Beach, where the small shore-based fleet and a handful of black-painted huts give way to a couple of Martello towers and the forbidding Hythe Ranges (a Ministry of Defence firing range). In the distance, the bay curves round to Dungeness. If the weather behaves, you can eat in front of *Griggs of Hythe*, the fishmongers on the beach. *Hythe Bay Seafood Restaurant & Bar*, east along the prom, is another beachside option; from here you can watch the antics of the sailing club.

The High Street is a pedestrian-friendly, old-fashioned high street, with a good mix of businesses, including a clutch of antiques and junk shops, and a chocolate shop, *Hendricks of Hythe*. Pubs and cafés are well represented, too; and there's even a microbrewery, The *Potting Shed*. Behind the splendid town hall (built 1794), there's a footpath leading up to St Leonard's Church and crypt. The town has been around for a while – the church dates from the eleventh century. Hythe was a Cinque Port, and the canal and the Martello towers show its strategic importance in the Napoleonic Wars; follow the short Heritage Trail round town for more information.

DUNGENESS

The shingle wilderness first popularised by Derek Jarman in the 1990s has changed a lot since his day – it's been spruced up, and is rarely without visitors – but it remains a strange and atmospheric place. A snaking line of pylons leads to the enormous nuclear power complex, which dwarfs everything, even the two lighthouses and the Martello tower. Low-slung houses pepper the landscape, many of them designer versions of the tar-painted dwellings they replaced, but there are still shacks, caravans and converted railway carriages in the mix. *Prospect Cottage*, Jarman's house and garden, can be seen on the road leading down to the power station. It may not look like it, but the whole area is a nature reserve, home to a wide variety of plants and wildlife – many of them rare – so visitors are asked to keep to designated paths. There's an RSPB bird sanctuary nearby, too, which is also the home of the concrete *Sound Mirrors*, a striking set of decommissioned listening devices; the RSPB holds occasional tours.

Fishing boats sit on the shingle surrounded by old shipping containers; the catch can be bought at the nearby *Fish Hut*, or eaten at the adjacent kiosk. There are a few boardwalks leading down to the water, but you can't swim here – signs warn of strong currents and 'deep cold water'. Go to the edge of the undulating shingle for views of the white cliffs at Folkestone and Dover; in season, you can climb to the top of the *Old Lighthouse* to get your bearings.

For a bleak, reflective, landscape-centred walk, come on a midweek day in winter. For a less desolate day out, visit in summer, when the coastal plants are in bloom and the Romney, Hythe & Dymchurch line is running a full timetable. The narrow-gauge railway terminates in a visitor centre, which has a café with outdoor seating and a kiosk branded 'Ales by the Rails' selling Romney Marsh beer. Both the *Britannia* pub and the *Pilot Inn* are open year-round; the latter does a roaring trade in fish and chips and has a big screen plotting the course of ships in the Channel.

CAMBER & RYE

The beauty of Camber Sands is hidden behind a range of dunes – and the first sight of the vast expanse of sand and sea is a real thrill. The magnificent beach is worth a trip at any time of year, but if you want the place to yourself, visit during the winter. Once the weather takes a turn for the better, everyone from kitesurfers to sunbathers wants a piece of the golden sands. There *is* space for everyone, but don't come on a hot bank-holiday weekend (you'll be sitting in grid-locked traffic rather than on the beach). The beach is backed by a village, a Pontin's (which has a useful shop) and a caravan park; after many years of being off the radar, Camber has been rediscovered, and some stylish, eco-friendly coastal homes are beginning to appear. Restaurant recommendations start and finish with the *Gallivant* hotel (so book well ahead); The *Owl* offers pub grub. Most people take a picnic or grab an ice-cream or a snack from either of the two caffs on the beach, but for a proper coffee, walk a little further east to Broomhill Sands and *Tatner's Kitchen*, a mobile café parked next to the Kitesurf Centre. There are also a few shops selling buckets and spades – this is a great beach for sandcastle building – and other seaside paraphernalia.

The dunes look impressive – and provide welcome shelter when the wind is brisk – but are vulnerable to wear and tear from holidaymakers and their bad habits (littering, barbecuing and trampling delicate plants). Part of the dune system is designated an SSSI (Site of Special Scientific Interest); it's fine to explore, just keep to the footpaths. Eastwards, the dunes peter out, to be replaced by a promenade that stretches to the army firing range at Lydd; the giant rocks that form part of the sea defence here are imported granite, all the way from Norway.

For retail therapy, a choice of restaurants and bars, and a train back to London, head for Rye, the handsome town that was once on the coast but now lies a couple of miles inland. You can walk or cycle to Rye along a cycle track (not along the beach – that end of Camber Sands ends abruptly with the River Rother and Rye Harbour), or hop on the bus. Check out *Lamb House* (both Henry James and EF Benson lived here, though not together). Pubs run from the smart bar at *The George in Rye* hotel to the food-focused *Globe Inn Marsh*; the *Ypres Castle Inn* is a must-visit in good weather for the view from the beer garden, while the revamped *Standard Inn* is a favourite for its open fire and warm welcome. The *White House* and the *Fig* are classy cafés. Wander in and around the High Street and Mermaid Street, admiring the mish-mash of historic buildings and the cobbled lanes. A range of independent shops includes the wonderful *Glass Etc, Jane Wicks*

Kitchenalia and *Grammar School Records*. The *Kino* cinema is a godsend on rainy days.

Heading west out of town, Harbour Road leads to Rye Harbour, a tucked-away spot with a friendly pub, the *William the Conqueror*, and a lovely walk along the canal-like River Rother, beside a nature reserve, to the beach. Once at the seafront, you can walk (west) for miles – all the way to Hastings and beyond.

WINCHELSEA BEACH

The two Winchelseas – Winchelsea and Winchelsea Beach – are a mile apart in distance and much further apart in ambience. Much of Winchelsea Beach village is hidden behind Sea Road – lanes and footpaths leading off the road run down to a long sweep of shingle, divided by low wooden groynes, and with far-reaching views around Rye Bay. Sand is revealed at low tide, and a sea wall runs along the beach. You can walk or cycle east towards Rye Harbour, past the nature reserve and the thought-provoking *Mary Stanford Lifeboat House memorial*, or west to Pett Level, where as well as the shingle beach there are some swanky houses to admire. The cliffs to the west mark Fairlight and the start of the Hastings Country Park. There are a handful of shops in Winchelsea Beach, but of most interest to visitors is The *Ship*, which houses a restaurant/bar with plenty of garden seating and a deli with a great butcher's counter.

Up on the hill, Winchelsea is impossibly cute. A medieval grid system is lined with picture-perfect houses from several eras, and there's an impressive church and the ruins of an ancient town wall. It used to be an important place, a Cinque Port and a centre for wine trading (there are close to 50 ancient cellars in the town), but as the River Brede dwindled, so did Winchelsea. Its raised position means glorious views in all directions;

stand at The Lookout near Strand Gate for views of the sea, Camber Castle and the Royal Military Canal (which terminates just beyond here at Cliff End). An upmarket village store, *Winchelsea Farm Kitchen*, can provide hot drinks; there's also a pub, the *New Inn,* and an interesting shop, *Black Cat Gallery* (art and collectables). A bus links the two villages.

HASTINGS

Once Hastings has got under your skin, you'll keep coming back – maybe for good (the town has a big population of DFLs). It's an addictive mix of seaside fun, artistic activity and proper working town. Newbies should get their bearings from the viewpoint of the splendid resurrected pier – winner of the 2017 RIBA Stirling Prize for architecture. From the pier, you can see the Country Park, perched on the cliff (easily accessible by East Hill Lift, one of two funiculars in Hastings) and a great place to blow away any cobwebs – from it you can walk for miles along the coastal path (this is also the route to the nudist beach at Fairlight Glen). The town's other funicular (the West Hill Cliff Railway) takes you up to the ruined castle and a green sward that's perfect for a picnic with a view, and for exercising children and dogs.

From the pier, the promenade leads west to St Leonards and east to the Old Town, and is easier to walk along than the sand and shingle beach. Just near the pier is the charming *Arthur Green's Antiques Centre* and a little area called America Ground, worth checking out for the dog boutique *Collared*, the *Bullet Coffee House* and the homewares store *Dyke & Dean* (above which is The *Printworks*, a bar and event space that's also a cool B&B). Behind this patch of bohemia is the modern town centre.

It's a short hop along the front to the Old Town, past amusement arcades, rock shops and the child-friendly funfair *Flamingo Park*. All ages will be tempted by *Hastings Adventure Golf*, which has three courses, including a pirate-themed one. Kids will love the miniature railway, which weaves along the front and through the distinctive black-painted net huts that signal the working end of the beach. This is the Stade; as well as the beach-based fishing fleet, the *Jerwood Gallery* (twentieth-century British art) and the atmospheric *Fishermen's Museum* are here. This is where to buy the recently landed catch, or have it with chips at *Maggie's*. Walk to the end of Rock A Nore Road to see the dramatic cliffs – and rockfalls – up close.

Just inland from the Stade is Hastings Old Town, where the action is concentrated on and around George Street and the High Street. It's a browser's paradise, with shops ranging from the delightfully chaotic *Roberts Rummage* and the *Yard* to stylised one-offs such as *AG Hendy & Co Home Store* (which also sometimes operates an idiosyncratic restaurant). For clothes and accessories, *Warp & Weft* is irresistible; *Capsule* is another fail-safe. Established gift shops include *Made in Hastings* and *Butlers Emporium; Hare & Hawthorn* bindery and bookshop has some lovely items, too.

The Old Town is blessed with a number of great pubs: the friendly, award-winning *Crown*, where the food just gets better and better; the vibey *Dragon Bar*, for vodka shots and Sunday lunches; the handsome, revamped *Albion*; and old-school *FILO* (First in Last Out), for real ale and a proper pub. *Petit Fi* café does great cakes, coffees and snacks. Picnics on the beach are easily catered for: try the *Blue Dolphin* for fish and chips, *Judges Bakery* for mighty sausage rolls and *Di Pola's* for ice-cream. Just watch out for marauding seagulls. The *Old Custom House* and *Rock A Nore Kitchen*, both fish and seafood specialists, are safe indoor bets. Away from the Old Town, *Billycan*, the stall on the pier, is good for a take-away coffee, while *Imperial*, a revamped boozer, justifies a short walk up Queen's Road for craft beer and wood-fired pizza. If you've made it this far, carry on for a few minutes to beautiful Alexandra Park – one of many green spaces dotted throughout the town.

You'll need more than a day trip to fully sample the after-dark activities – there's a thriving music scene, with regular gigs in venues ranging from the down-home *Jenny Lind Inn* to the atmospheric former church *St Mary in the Castle* and the multimedia *Palace*. Try to make time for a trip to the tiny independent *Electric Palace Cinema*, too. Hastings loves an excuse to dress up and party, and throughout the year there are events galore, from Jack in the Green (the early May Bank Holiday weekend) to Hastings' bonfire night (held in October, and where the procession is as much fun as the fireworks).

ST LEONARDS-ON-SEA

Attached to Hastings, but very much its own place, St Leonards is worthy of a day trip in its own right. Architecture fans should make it a priority: it was built as a seaside resort in the nineteenth century by James Burton (responsible for the villas around Regent's Park in London) and his son Decimus, and as a result has some notable houses, not to mention a gracious park (St Leonards Gardens, good for seagull-free picnics). The most striking structure in town, however, is the Art Deco apartment block Marine Court, which resembles an ocean liner and dominates the seafront. If buildings don't do it for you, there are still plenty of diversions, and it's an easy walk along the promenade to Hastings or, going east, to Bexhill, home to the striking De La Warr Pavilion.

The beach is a mix of shingle and sand, divided by groynes, and it's enjoyed by everyone from schools of language students to lone dog walkers. You can shelter from the rain under the lower deck of the promenade (on the walk to Hastings, check out the 1930s, a Bottle Alley, named after the pieces of glass bottles embedded in the concrete).

The town is served by two train stations, and it's a short hop from the Warrior Square station to the shops and cafés on Norman, London and King's Roads.

Omega is a small shop/gallery filled with covetable goodies; *Sideshow Interiors* (twentieth-century furniture and decorative bits) and *Wayward* (vintage haberdashery) are also wallet-openers. There are plenty of junk shops and antiques galleries to poke around in, too, notably the vintage-clothes store *Xanadu*.

Coffee stops include *Kassa* (incongruously also an opticians) and homewares store *Shop*. Multi-tasking is clearly a thing: *Kino-Teatr* is a small independent cinema and gallery with a good café attached. Serious eats can be had at *St Clements*, a classy neighbourhood restaurant with a modern European menu and a weekend brunch, and at *Graze on Grand*, a winning blend of wine bar, bottle shop and gallery. More casual is the ramshackle *Love Café*; *Half Man! Half Burger!* has juicy meat and veggie burgers; *Café Gratitude* is the vegan diner of choice; while modernised pub The *St Leonard* is the go-to drinking haunt.

BEXHILL

Visitors come to Bexhill for the De La Warr Pavilion, but there's more to this little seaside town than its 1930s landmark. The town centre is tired but in the process of rejuvenation. There are some beautiful old shopfronts, and lots of family-run businesses, with fewer chains than on the average high street – though Wetherspoon occupies what was the Picture Playhouse cinema. Lovers of junk and charity shops will be in seventh heaven – try St Leonards Road, Western Road and Sackville Road. A few twenty-first-century outlets are starting to appear: The *Driftwood* is a café with rooms for rent, and makes for a great coffee stop close to the seafront; *Rocksalt-on-Sea* is a friendly brasserie/bar (which also has rooms) opposite the De La Warr. Also handy for the Pavilion is *Di Paolo*, the must-visit ice-cream parlour.

Of course, the town's crowning glory is the Grade I listed *De La Warr Pavilion*, which was built in 1935 and occupies a prime position on the seafront. It's a gallery, venue and café (with lots of roof-terrace seating); in front are landscaped lawns, a child-friendly water feature and an outdoor performance space, all with views out to sea.

The promenade at this point has a few shops and cafés, plus sailing and rowing clubs, and a delightful row of houses, Marina Court Avenue, built in Edwardian

Moghul style. The beach is shingle, spotted with sea kale, and there are stretches of sand at low tide. There's a fine view all the way round the bay to Eastbourne, and the shore is quiet compared with local resorts. Walk east, past beach huts and alongside the railway line to St Leonards, four miles away. Head west, along a promenade transformed by strikingly modern beach shelters and modish municipal planting, and you'll reach Cooden Beach. There's a station here, so you can always catch the train back to Bexhill. A long-distance path, the 1066 Country Walk, threads out of Bexhill into farm and woodland.

The town's other claim to fame is as the 'Birthplace of British Motor Racing'. The first motor race took place along De La Warr Parade in 1902, and petrolheads can follow a trail that includes a motor heritage gallery at *Bexhill Museum*.

Bexhill

PEVENSEY BAY

Looking at the simple shingle and sand beach, lined with weathered wooden groynes, it's hard to imagine that the course of English history changed dramatically here when William the Conqueror landed in 1066. The wider view takes in the cliffs at Hastings in the east, round to Eastbourne Harbour in the west, with Beachy Head and the South Downs in the distance. Off-season, the beach can be almost deserted, apart from dog walkers and birds. Besides the ever-present gulls, cormorants fish just off the beach and turnstones run around on the shoreline. There are a couple of year-round beach cafés, and an ice-cream kiosk in season.

Pevensey Bay is an unassuming spot, with a hotch-potch of dwellings that includes Edwardian villas, Martello towers, bungalows, static caravans and a 1930s beachfront marvel, The *Sandcastle*. Much of the housing is strung out along the coast, though Eastbourne Road is where most shops and cafés can be found.

Architecture hounds should make a detour to check out Pevensey Bay's 1930s *Beachlands Estate*; everyone should follow the footpath across the fields to Pevensey, to see the romantic-looking medieval castle. The ruins contain the remnants of a Roman fort, and the complex provides an attractive shortcut between Pevensey and the adjoining village, Westham. Both villages are pretty, with a choice of pubs and tea rooms; Westham also has the *Swan* fish and chip shop. From Pevensey, the 1066 Country Walk footpath leads deep into the Pevensey Levels: a large area of marshland marked by drainage channels, designated an SSSI and full of wetland birds. It's a very distinctive, tranquil place, miles away from main roads and noise and, like Pevensey Bay, perfect for a contemplative walk.

EASTBOURNE

Eastbourne's appeal for jaded Londoners is twofold: the *Towner Art Gallery* and Beachy Head. The Towner Art Gallery, housed in a Rick Mather-designed building set back from the seafront, is known for its collection of modern British art, particularly work by local boy Eric Ravilious. Magnificent Beachy Head is a couple of miles away – head west out of town for one of the most spectacular walks in the south of England.

It doesn't hurt that Eastbourne has a fine seafront, stretching for miles and lined with gardens, amusements (children will love *Treasure Island* adventure park), an attractive Victorian pier, a Martello tower (the *Wish Tower*) and the *Redoubt Fortress*. Walk along the pier for impressive views of the white cliffs. The Art Deco bandstand lays claim to being the busiest in the UK and has a varied programme of musical events, plus fireworks in high season. The seafront *Grand Hotel* is painted icing-sugar white and is very grand indeed; it offers a glimpse of Eastbourne in its Victorian prime. Shelter here with a smart afternoon tea in inclement weather.

The beach is shingle (and sand when the tide is out), and the main drag is populated by cafés and stalls selling ice-cream and snacks. The *Western View* café, near The *Wish Tower*, has lots of outdoor tables and a menu that encompasses beans on toast and glasses of prosecco. East past the pier, just off the seafront, is The *Beach Kitchen*, known for its slap-up breakfasts. Ice-cream in retro surroundings isn't hard to find – both *Fusciardi's* and *Favo'Loso* are sundae specialists.

The town centre is nowhere near as splendid as the promenade or the grand avenues running down to the seafront, but it has all the basics; charity-shop foragers will have a field day. The Little Chelsea neighbourhood just to the west of the railway station has more independent shops and cafés, mostly concentrated on Grove Road, including modish burger joint *Half Man! Half Burger!* and impressive second-hand bookstore *Camilla's Bookshop*. The *Dolphin* pub on nearby South Street is worth a visit, too. Further west, towards Beachy Head, is the Meads, an attractive cluster of roads, one of which, Meads Street, holds the *Black Cat Tearooms* and The *Ship Inn* (the beer garden is worth remembering for sunny days). The start (or finish) of the South Downs Way is at this end of town – Beachy Head itself is two miles along the trail. These cliffs are a great vantage point for watching the annual airshow in August.

Eastbourne

SEAFORD

Sleepy Seaford is surrounded by some of the loveliest countryside in Sussex. Footpaths lead out of town in all directions, but the most dramatic of these runs east along the cliff to Cuckmere Haven (the scenic flood plain immortalised by painter Eric Ravilious) and on to the Seven Sisters. Fans of Sussex artist Eric Slater can follow the Slater Trail – many of the views are little changed since he captured them in the 1930s.

The town itself has a long sweep of pebble beach, given drama by Seaford Head to the east and Newhaven Harbour in the distant west. The seafront is refreshingly low-key. There are no funfairs or amusements, just a couple of beach kiosks, one of which, *Frankie's*, has deck-chairs and a sandpit. A well-preserved Martello tower houses the *Seaford Museum*. Most shops and cafés are a five-minute walk from the beach, on and around Broad, Church and High Streets. You won't go hungry: there are several chippies, lots of pubs, cafés of all persuasions, and some good all-day options, notably the *Grumpy Chef* and *Front Room*. Shops tend to be independents and include a toy shop and a haberdasher's alongside a few modish gift shops – charity-shop trawlers will be kept busy.

If you want to see Seaford in a different light, come for Seaford Bonfire – it's not as full-on as the one in nearby Lewes, though the revels do involve a costumed bonfire procession and a firework display.

NEWHAVEN

With its working harbour and industry, Newhaven is one for lovers of off-kilter seaside. The road to the beach goes past a marina, several boatyards and some sturdy vessels, and ends in a car park just west of the harbour mouth. There's a pub just before the car park, but otherwise that's it for creature comforts. It's fabulously bleak on days when the wind whips the sea high in the air over the breakwater. This wall protects the harbour and encloses a sandy beach – which is, sadly, off-limits (it's owned by the port authority); there's a lighthouse at the end. On the other side of the breakwater is an undulating pebble beach, backed by white cliffs and dotted with sea kale. There are a few weatherbeaten huts, and the remains of a radar defence unit built into the cliff. On the top of the cliffs is *Newhaven Fort*, once an important coastal defence and now a tourist attraction with a 1940s-themed tea room. A stroll along the top reveals further derelict defences, as well as amazing views.

Walk a couple of miles on the clifftop to reach Peacehaven – the town is an unlovely sprawl, but once there you can drop down to the Undercliff promenade, which runs alongside the startlingly white cliff-face. Here, the beach is a mix of shingle, sand and exposed chalk. Don't attempt to walk between Newhaven and Peacehaven along the beach, however tempting it looks at low tide – the sea can come in surprisingly fast.

The Sussex Ouse Valley Way long-distance path also goes through Newhaven; it passes on the eastern side of the harbour before running along the coast towards Seaford.

ROTTINGDEAN

An endearing combination of quaint, flint-walled village and no-frills seaside resort, Rottingdean is a one-off. The idyllic duck pond and picturesque black windmill are straight out of central casting. At the seafront, white cliffs tower over a concrete walkway, the Undercliff; the beach is a mix of shingle, sand and exposed chalk (so plenty of rock pools). It's a family- and dog-friendly place, with a lifeguard in season and a handy beachfront café, *Molly's*. There are a few more cafés, beach shops and so on above the beach, including *Sea Spray*. The seafront part of Rottingdean is divided from the village by the busy A27. Cross over for a pint in one of the old pubs or a slice of home-made cake in the delightful walled *Grange Tea Garden*. The Grange is also a small museum and gallery, and was once the home of painter Sir William Nicholson. The streets are full of beautiful houses, including those of Sir Edward Burne-Jones and Rudyard Kipling. The old gardens of Kipling's house are now a pretty public park. Grade II listed *St Margaret's Church* has an equally charming, wild, churchyard garden and seven stained-glass windows designed by Burne-Jones and made by William Morris and his firm.

There are walks out of Rottingdean straight out on to the Beacon Hill National Nature Reserve (part of the Downs), or you can walk along the Undercliff. Heading eastwards, the path goes to Saltdean, notable for its glorious 1930s Art Deco lido. Restored and reopened in 2017, it looks an absolute picture and is an easy 15-minute walk. In the other direction is Brighton, just three miles away.

BRIGHTON

The getaway of choice for Londoners who don't want to escape city life, Brighton pretty much has it all – apart from a sandy shore. There are shops, restaurants, cafés, pubs, nightclubs, music venues, cinemas, theatres, galleries, tourist attractions, casinos and parks, and there's no way you can cover it in a weekend, never mind a day trip.

The beach here is pebble, overlooked by a promenade, under which are arches containing shops and cafés. There's plenty of seafront – the walk from the border with Hove to Brighton Marina takes 50 minutes – but it's busy whatever the time of year; in summer it can be overwhelming. There are amusements and diversions galore: between the skeletal remains of the West Pier and the fun-packed Brighton (or Palace) Pier, there's a paddling pool, a bandstand, the i360, the sailing club, a basketball court, a giant sand pit and the *Fishing Museum*. And that's before you count the refreshments, with ice-creams, fish and chips, burgers, oysters, real ale and champagne jostling for attention. In season, the Volks Electric Railway runs from near Brighton Pier to just before Brighton Marina. The impressive Brighton Pier has rides and amusements for all ages, and is open year-round.

Since the Prince Regent gave the place his seal of approval in 1783, Brighton has been the leading resort on the south coast. The building spree that followed has left the town with gracious Regency architecture, and some lovely squares and crescents. The extraordinary Grade I listed *Royal Pavilion* is a must-visit; also handsome is nearby *Brighton Museum*, a rewarding refuge on a rainy day.

The little winding streets known as the Lanes date back to when the city was a fishing village. Shops here are mainly upmarket chains and jewellery stores. Things turn funkier and more interesting in the North Laine area, where the mix features independent boutiques such as *Sirene* and *Tidy Street General Store*, record and book stores and junk shops (of which *Snoopers Paradise* is the king). There are lots of separate shopping hubs, though: big-name chains around Churchill Square; vintage stores in Kemp Town; a clutch of lovely local shops around Seven Dials; and new ventures transforming the area in and around London Road.

Good coffee can be found everywhere; if in doubt, head for a branch of *Small Batch*. Most cuisines are covered: a host of veggie places includes the long-standing *Food for Friends* and *Terre à Terre*; good fish and seafood can be had at *Riddle & Finns*; and east Londoners will feel right at home at *Silo*.

Brighton's nightlife is vibrant, with a choice of pubs, clubs, music venues and theatres. For a big night out, *Brighton Dome* is a relatively intimate place to see a big-name performer; for a more low-key evening, drink Brighton-brewed beer at *North Laine Brewhouse* or *Brighton Bierhaus*. The city knows how to rise to a special occasion, too – come down for the Brighton Festival (May), Brighton Pride (August) or Artists Open Houses (May and December), among many other events.

HOVE

Hove goes from chic to suburban and grand to grotty in the space of a few yards, shape-shifting to be whatever kind of seaside experience you want it to be. It lacks the corporate hotels and full-on bustle of Brighton, but there's plenty to amuse: interesting arts venues such as The *Old Market*; a good selection of restaurants and pubs; plenty of beach space for everyone; and pottering opportunities galore. Often, the architecture is a treat: there are some lovely avenues running down to the sea, and majestic nineteenth-century squares such as Adelaide Crescent, Palmeira Square and Brunswick Square are stunning.

Wandering from one neighbourhood shopping area to the next gives you a crash course in Hove's varied architectural styles. It's easy to hop between one enclave and another. Clustered near Hove station are a few shops and cafés, including a branch of local coffee heroes *Small Batch* and two versions of *Wolfies*, one offering fish and chips, the other serving comfort food. South of here, between the station and the sea, is Blatchington Road, a regular high street dotted with charity shops and enlivened by the odd gem such as *Bobby & Dandy* vintage clothing. Portland Road, just to the west, has more independents, including *Wick Candle Boutique*. Further south-west, Richardson Road has a small but lovely bunch of cafés and one-off businesses. But the big hitter is Western Road – it's close to the beach, and has lots of restaurants and pubs, not to mention classy shops such as *City Books, Dowse Design* (art and design) and *i gigi* (two branches: one womenswear, one homewares and tea room).

Hove's long promenade is lined with brightly painted beach huts, and runs alongside several beaches, all pebbled and all looking pretty much the same; the groynes are sometimes concrete, sometimes wood; railings give way to concrete wall and back again. You won't go hungry – there are refreshment kiosks at regular intervals. Go west as far as Hove Lagoon and you'll hit a private beach and a small industrial estate; after that it's Portslade. The Lagoon offers watersports and is also home to the *Big Beach Café*, a skate park, a crazy-golf course, a paddling pool and a children's playground. The beach at this end is dog-friendly all year round. Walk far enough east and you're in Brighton – the divide between Hove and Brighton is generally agreed to be at the Peace Statue, just before the looming i360. The busiest area of the prom is around the King's Esplanade, blighted by the hulking King Alfred leisure centre and enhanced by *Marrocco's* home-made ice-cream, Hove Lawns and a few nineteenth-century houses – gracious reminders of the resort's grand beginnings.

Hove has enough of a drinking scene to make a night of it; if you want to eat in one of the rated gastropubs, such as The *Ginger Pig* or The *Foragers*, book ahead.

SHOREHAM-
BY-SEA

There's an intriguing geography to Shoreham-by-Sea.
The beach lies on a shingle spit; the River Adur runs
behind it, splitting Shoreham in two. A modern swing
bridge, the Adur Ferry Bridge, links the busy town
centre with the more relaxed beach-side development.
Shoreham Harbour, to the east of the town, marks
the start of an industrial strip of coast that runs up
to Hove and gives the resort some grit. The old town
centre rewards browsing, and has more quality coffee
shops and tea rooms than seems possible – *Ginger &*
Dobbs and *Real Patisserie* can be found on East Street,
a pretty thoroughfare running down to the ancient
Church of St Mary de Haura. The *Crown & Anchor* has a
terrace that overlooks the river and the bridge. There
are plenty of boats to admire on the Adur, ranging
from dinghies to yachts and including an assortment
of houseboats, which are marooned on the mudflats
when the tide goes out.

To reach the seafront, cross the Adur Ferry Bridge
and follow Lower Beach Road to the end. The beach
has a safe swimming area (away from the kitesurfers),
a long boardwalk running eastwards, and a great array
of coastal plants. West is Lancing; in the other direction, the beach ends at the mouth of the river, with
views of a Victorian stone lighthouse, the port and the

remains of *Shoreham Redoubt*, an 1857 fort. Walk out on the harbour arm; the panorama across the bay takes in Brighton and the white cliffs around Newhaven, round to Worthing and beyond in the west, with a wind farm straight ahead. Equally fascinating is the collection of swanky holiday houses lining the beach – some of them even have swimming pools.

WORTHING

In the latter half of the eighteenth century, Worthing was quite the destination resort, leaving the town with a legacy of gracious Georgian crescents, later supplemented by Victorian villas and 1920s buildings. Although always outshone by its flashier neighbour Brighton, these days Worthing is increasingly seen as the more relaxed, leafier, cheaper option, both to live in and to visit.

A spacious, well-maintained seafront, where the promenade runs seamlessly onto the beach, is backed by an attractive mix of hotels, bars and houses; the shingle and sand beach is divided by weathered groynes and stretches far into the distance. The pier, an Art Deco edifice stretching over 960 feet into the waves, is a stunner and holds two cafés and a neat little amusement arcade; sit at the end of the pier in the *Southern Pavilion* café (also used for gigs) for magnificent views in any weather.

The busy town centre isn't without character and has enough independent shops and cafés to keep things interesting. Just west of the centre, along and around Rowlands Road, there's a strip of browsable shops, including second-hand treasure trove *Badger's Books*, vintage and modern homewares store *Warehouse 13*, and cake shop/café *Baked*. It's a short stroll into the centre for one-off boutiques The *Griffin, Sneaker* and

Retro Daisy; as well as the shops, look out for *Desert Quartet*, the impressive set of heads on Liverpool Gardens made by sculptor Elisabeth Frink.

There's a slew of decent eateries, too, including The *Woods Burger Kitchen, Fiordilatte* for pizzas and, near the East Beach promenade, *CrabShack*. Ice-creams can be had at *Guiseppe's Lite* and *Boho Gelato*; grab a coffee at *Black Crow* (handy for Worthing railway station) or *Small Batch*. Finding a pub or a bar isn't a problem either, from the *Anchored in Worthing* micro-brewery and pub to the *Beach House* seafront bar.

There's plenty to keep all ages entertained, from the crazy golf and ultra-modern *Splashpoint* pool to the two independent cinemas: the *Dome* (Grade II listed and first opened in 1911) and the *Connaught* (also a theatre). Don't be fooled by signs for the Lido, though – the open-air pool was built over in 1990.

Worthing is on the edge of the South Downs National Park, and both the South Downs Way and the Monarch's Way long-distance footpaths run behind the town. The best direction to walk along the seafront is westwards to Goring-by-Sea, where your reward is the *Sea Lane Café*.

EAST BEACH
LITTLEHAMPTON

Most Londoners will have registered the existence of Littlehampton when the *East Beach Café* opened in 2007. Designed by Thomas Heatherwick, it's a unique flowing structure in rusted steel that somehow looks just right on the exposed seafront; big windows mean every table has a view of the waves. You can eat in (book ahead) or order a take-away; the menu is mostly fish and seafood, and they do a mean fish and chips. The owners of the café also came up with the idea for the crazy benches lining the promenade. But well before the café launch, families-in-the-know holidayed here. The beach is great for children, with lots of sand revealed at low tide and lifeguards on duty. The road is well away from the beach, on the far side of a huge green sward, and the wide concrete promenade is perfect for scooters, bikes and skate-boards as well as pedestrians. The town has several well-maintained municipal parks and a boating lake. The small-scale Harbour Park complex, where the river meets the beach, has a soft play area for small children, as well as amusement arcades and fairground rides – not to mention a bronze statue of Billy Smart, circus owner. Windsurfers, kitesurfers and surfers also make use of the coast here – it's often breezy. Walkers not wanting to cross the river must head east, towards

Rustington, watching the offshore wind farm fade in and out of view as the weather changes.

The River Arun, which splits the beaches at Little-hampton, gives the resort another dimension. The riverside walkway takes you past a harbour lined with all manner of boats, a few cafés, *Riverside Fish* (a fresh-fish hut) and the *Look & Sea Visitor Centre*, which has a viewing tower and a café with outdoor seating, *Harbour Lights*. The town centre is quaint but struggling, with a lot of boarded-up shopfronts; apart from the enticing *Fireside Bookshop*, there's not much to distract trippers from the pleasures of the riverside and seashore.

WEST BEACH
LITTLEHAMPTON &
CLIMPING

West Beach Littlehampton is a very different prospect to East Beach, even though they're both technically in the same town. Surreally, you can see the castle turrets of the amusement park just across the River Arun, but the dividing water means it's a 40-minute walk, an irregular ferry ride, or a three-mile car ride between the two. This side is wilder, more expansive and a lot emptier. Stand at the harbour mouth and watch the currents struggle as the river water meets the incoming tide. The beach is backed by sand dunes (designated an SSSI and a rare sight on this stretch of coast). On inclement days, you might be sharing the beach with a handful of dog walkers (dogs are welcome all year round), and even in the height of summer it's easy to escape any hustle and bustle. The only structure here is the *West Beach Café*; designed by Asif Khan, it's the less showy sibling of the *East Beach Café*. Don't rely on it for sustenance – if there aren't many customers, it may close early (even in August). You can park at West Beach, but it's more interesting to walk from the town, over the footbridge and along the working side of the river, past boatyards and a yacht club.

Along the beach, it's a mile and a half to Climping; at low tide there's enough sand to make this an easy

prospect. You can do it over the pebbles but it's more of a workout. However you manage the trek, it's worth doing, as this is the least-developed coastline in the area, and the dunes give way to woods and fields as you get to Climping Beach. Once there, the reward is a slap-up tea at faux-medieval *Bailiffscourt Hotel* (book ahead) or a pint at the *Black Horse Inn*.

BOGNOR REGIS

The name makes Bognor sound much grander than it actually is. The 'Regis' was bestowed on the small town after George V stayed here; these days, there's not much that's regal about the resort, but it does provide a good day out. It was almost called Hothamton, after Richard Hotham, the man who transformed it from a fishing village to a seaside destination. In the end, his name lives on in Hotham Park only, and there are just a few remnants of the glory days of the resort still standing.

The pebble beach is backed by a ribbon of prom-enade, which reaches the suburbs of Aldwick in the west and Felpham in the east. In season, a little train runs along the seafront and children can access the giant sandpit. There are kiosks for snacks, ice-creams and deckchairs, a stubby pier with an amusement arcade, a bandstand, crazy golf and a Butlin's. You can't miss the holiday camp – it dominates the area east of the pier – and the complex includes a funfair and an indoor water park (day tickets are available). Just past Butlin's, going east, is the likeable *Lobster Pot* café – the suntrap garden is the perfect spot to watch the waves, summer or winter.

The town centre is unremarkable, but there are lots of caffs. *Grandad's Front Room* is the most eccentric of the charity shops; *Heygates Bookshop* is also worth a look

– the shop is bigger than it first appears and is rammed floor to ceiling with second-hand books.

A short walk from the beach, Hotham Park provides a charming, shady alternative to the shore. The 22 acres hold a miniature railway, a boating pond, a wild-life area and a superior café (owned by the people who run the Lobster Pot – this branch has a pizza oven).

SELSEY

Selsey is at the end of the road on the Manhood Peninsula, and gives every impression of being its own little world. Even in summer when the holidaymakers arrive, any razzmatazz is limited to the Bunn Leisure Holiday Park, just west of town. The old-fashioned town centre is set apart from the beach, separated by wide residential streets. Stroll between the two and check out the 1930s villas and the thatched cottages; elsewhere, the seaside bungalow rules. The basics – a butcher's, a baker's and a few eccentric charity shops, and several cafés and pubs – can be found on the High Street; The *Crab Pot* is a micropub and the *Riviera* does a brisk trade in fry-ups.

Coastal footpaths are patchy here, which is a shame as the views of the sea and the Isle of Wight are fabulous; walking around the tip of the peninsula means a scramble over the groynes at low tide, as the footpath diverts inland. The best stretch of promenade is along East Beach, past the state-of-the-art RNLI station and shop, towards the marshlands of Pagham Harbour and birdwatching heaven. On the way is a blue plaque to Eric Coates, who, inspired by the view, composed 'By the Sleepy Lagoon' – known today as the theme tune to *Desert Island Discs*. Fishing boats bob up and down on the water near the lifeboat station; *Potters* sells coffee and freshly caught seafood out of a smart kiosk.

This beach is shingle – there's more sand just round the peninsula on Hillfield Road Beach.

Selsey's most notable landmark, the pier-like offshore lifeboat house and jetty, was dismantled in 2017. A spanking-new lifeboat house sits just inland of East Beach; it's handsome – and vital – but it doesn't have the romance of the vanished structure.

EAST WITTERING

Together, East Wittering and West Wittering are known as the Witterings; though next to each other, they don't have much in common, but they complement each other nicely. West Wittering may have the looks, but East Wittering has the amenities. It also has the rare distinction of being a Thankful Village, one of the few villages in England where all the men who fought in World War I returned – there's a plaque in *St Anne's Church*.

Not that the beach at East Wittering is to be sniffed at – it just suffers by comparison with carefully preserved West Wittering. Banked shingle divided by wooden groynes gives way to expansive stretches of sand, appreciated by everyone from surfers to sandcastle-builders and, out of season, dog walkers. Ice-creams and fish and chips are within easy reach. Most shops, cafés and pubs can be found on Shore Road and Cakeham Road. At the beach end of Shore Road is The *Shore Inn* and a sizeable kiosk selling drinks and ice-creams; you might be lucky and catch the little hut selling fresh fish, too. A grassy area has benches positioned to make the most of the views out to sea and over to the Isle of Wight. Walk east round Bracklesham Bay to *Billy's on the Beach* for coffee and substantial snacks. The café is open year round, and there's plenty of space indoors for when the sun doesn't shine. The houses behind the beach are a classic seaside hotch-potch; elsewhere in the village, the bungalow is king. To see how the other half lives, stroll west along the grass and shingle footpath to West Wittering.

WEST WITTERING

The beach here is a knockout. It's thanks to the West Wittering Preservation Trust that the coastline around the village has escaped the over-development that blights much of the West Sussex coast. A group of locals banded together and bought the land in 1952, and the Trust still runs the place and operates the only car park. Once through the car park, dunes and beach huts give way to a stretch of pale sand lightly sprinkled with shells and pebbles. When the tide goes out, a large expanse of glistening sand is revealed beyond the wooden groynes. Inevitably, it's a honeypot destination, drawing everyone from horse riders and dog walkers to swimmers and windsurfers (there's a windsurfing and kitesurfing club at the main entrance to the beach).

For something a little wilder, walk to East Head, at the western end of the beach; owned by the National Trust, it's designated an SSSI. A sand and shingle spit backed by salt marsh, the area is a haven for wildlife, from seals to migrating birds. On any beach walk, you can see the Isle of Wight, watch yachts at play and follow container ships as they go past on their way to Portsmouth. For a longer hike, follow the New Lipchis Way past East Head, and along the coast to West Itchenor and beyond.

Refreshment options are limited (a picnic is the best plan) – there's a café next to the car park and another,

The *Landing*, in the village, a ten-minute walk from the beach. West Wittering village is worth exploring – it's very pretty, with thatched houses and flint cottages – but for a choice of shops, head to East Wittering. The route, an easy stroll on a grassy path behind the beach, takes you past a collection of exclusive dwellings – far too grand to be called beach houses – overlooking the sea.

Out of season, it's possible to have long solitary walks in West Wittering, but in summer the beach gets busy and the road gets even busier – there's only one route to and from the sea and inevitably there are long queues. Cyclists can avoid this by taking the 11-mile Salterns cycle route from Chichester.

FURTHER AFIELD

If you have a little more time on your hands, these are places worth exploring for a weekend getaway or an overnight stay …

BOURNEMOUTH

As a seaside destination with an urban, studenty vibe, Bournemouth can give Brighton a run for its money, with everything from independent coffee roasters to club nights. The town grew during the nineteenth century from almost nothing to become one of England's major holiday destinations; initially, visitors came for their health, but soon huge numbers came just for fun, as they do today. Entertainments aside, this buzzy resort is made special by its magnificent beach and luxuriant Victorian landscaping. The long coastal cliffs, dense with vegetation and interrupted at intervals by chines (steep valleys), form the perfect backdrop to miles of beautiful sand, lightly speckled with pebbles and shells. Pine trees and palms are everywhere, and the parks and gardens are kept just-so.

The promenade is at beach level, and it's a lovely 30-minute walk from the all-action town pier (rides, amusements and a zip wire) to the unadorned concrete Boscombe Pier. For much of the year, a land train trundles the distance, too. The colour-coordinated council beach huts lining the route are a delight, and many of them are for hire by the day or week. Spot the plaque identifying the first municipal beach hut in the UK. Zigzag paths lead up to the clifftop, where the views of the bay are even better; there are three cliff lifts (West, East and Fisherman's Walk) but at the time of writing the East Cliff lift was out of commission after a bad rockslide. Much of the beach is designated a Coastal Activity Park – activities on offer include volleyball and bouldering – and surfers and kitesurfers make the most of the water all year round.

Clustered around the main pier are restaurants and cafés, and an aquarium. Just inland is the mighty *Pavilion Theatre*, a 1920s venue for big-name shows, and, up on the clifftop, the charming *Russell-Cotes Art Gallery & Museum* – a must for aficionados of Victorian art. Lovely Lower Gardens (one of several Grade II listed parks) links the town centre to the seafront, and has a handsome bandstand and an aviary. Devotees of *Frankenstein* should know that Mary Shelley is buried close by, in the churchyard of St Peter's.

Bournemouth town centre, based around the Square, is a more characterful shopping hub than found in many resorts, and an independent spirit survives in the likes of *South Coast Roast* coffee shop, but inevitably chains dominate. For a more alternative vibe and some pleasant mooching, head inland from Boscombe Pier to Christchurch Street. This long strip has charity and second-hand shops, notably *Clobber* (vintage clothing), The *Crooked Book* (books, coffee and bric-a-brac) and *Claire's Collectables* (china heaven in a Victorian arcade), and some appealing cafés, including *Little Pickle Deli, Café Boscanova* and *Coffee & Dice* (for board games). If you've got a few days, other suburbs, such as Southbourne and Westbourne, are worth exploring, too. Or head west along the front to millionaire's enclave

Sandbanks – from here, there's a chain ferry over to the beautiful National Trust beach at Studland; the walk to the ferry takes just over an hour from Bournemouth Pier. In the other direction, about an hour's walk from Boscombe Pier, lies the nature reserve at Hengistbury Head.

HUNSTANTON

It's two resorts for the price of one here: Old Hunstanton village has a wholesome air, while Hunstanton town offers out-and-out seaside fun. The Victorian seaside resort, conceived by local Henry Le Strange, soon eclipsed the original village. Well-maintained formal gardens and a bandstand remain, but the pier has perished; the resort faces west (unusually for Norfolk), so, delightfully, the sun sets over the sea.

Both Hunstantons face a huge expanse of beach, which disappears when the tide is high. It's an easy walk between the two. From Old Hunstanton, apart from the decommissioned lighthouse and a small café, the clifftop is a green sward until the *Salad Bowl Café*, landscaped gardens, putting green and crazy golf signify a change of tempo. Down at beach level, dunes dotted with seagrass and beach huts give way to striped cliffs (a combination of chalk and the Norfolk carrstone, which gives the local cottages their distinctive look); the sand is mixed with shingle and shells, and at low tide there are lots of rock pools. Closer to Hunstanton, there's the hull of an old trawler and an other-worldly host of seaweed- and lichen-covered boulders to navigate before a more regulated stretch of sand, staked out by old wooden groynes, appears.

The town centre is small, but packed with cafés and fish and chip restaurants. Going west, the promenade is lined with amusement arcades, an indoor swimming pool and funfair rides. These days, the resort not only attracts trippers, but also kitesurfers (who love the long stretches of shallow water and the breeze) and birdwatchers. There are RSPB reserves at Titchwell and Snettisham, but plenty of species can be spotted on the beach and nesting in the cliffs. The Wash has a large colony of seals, too; in season, there are trips to see them aboard the amphibious *Wash Monster*.

Walkers can start the Norfolk Coast Path in Hunstanton; follow it for a couple of miles to Holme-next-the-Sea and there's another option, the cross-country Peddars Way. Walk as far as you like along the coast – the efficient Coasthopper bus service will return you to Hunstanton.

HOLKHAM

The beach at Holkham is something special. Pine woods and sand dunes provide an elegant setting; and on the walk towards the beach along the snaking boardwalk, anticipation mounts. Miles of sand stretch ahead; there's always room for everyone, even on the sunniest of days – it's just a question of how far you're prepared to walk. This strip of coast is kept pristine by the Holkham Estate, which also owns nearby *Holkham Hall* (the house, gardens and parkland are open to visitors for much of the year). Even though the beach seems isolated, getting here is easy – the hassle-free way to arrive is on the Coasthopper bus, but there's a big car park, too, and the Norfolk Coast Path runs behind the beach.

At the end of the boardwalk, a raised viewing point showcases the scene. Beyond a patch of salt marsh lies the beach proper, used by horse riders, birdwatchers, dog walkers and legions of holidaying families. It's a tonic to be here, whatever the weather; there's a sense of freedom that comes with the sheer amount of space, and children can run to their heart's content. It's enchanting, even on overcast winter days when the sea seems to meld with the sky.

A picnic is a good idea, especially if you've set up camp in a remote spot; refreshments are limited to a seasonal snack van at the end of the car park on Lady

Anne's Drive. Otherwise, it's the *Victoria* pub-with-rooms (book ahead) or the *Courtyard Café*, back in Holkham Park next to a clutch of shops guaranteed to separate the middle classes from their money. Or you could walk a couple of miles along the beach to Wells-next-the-Sea, home to a more traditional sort of seaside village and the closest spot for fish and chips.

SHERINGHAM

Sheringham has an old-fashioned appeal, from the steam trains on the Poppy Line railway to the annual carnival in August. What was a fishing village grew – a little – and today it's an attractive flint-and-red-brick resort with a model-yacht pond, a putting green and the *Peter Coke Shell Gallery*. There are a handful of kiosks and cafés, a few boats and some pastel-coloured beach huts, but otherwise it's all about the beach. Banks of shingle and rocks give way to first-class sand, perfect for sandcastles, with lots of space for beach games, and washed clean with every tide. The wooden groynes mean plenty of rockpools when the water recedes. Sea defence is taken seriously here, with the concrete sea wall bolstered by huge boulders – damage from the 2013 sea surge is a reminder of how vulnerable this coast is.

Station Road, the High Street and Church Street form the heart of town, and are lined with family-run businesses, including the *Chocolate Box, P & J Scotter Fishmongers* (for local crab) and ironmongers-cum-department store *Blyth & Wright*. The charity and junk shops are an individual bunch, great for an afternoon's trawling. Sheringham's cafés punch above their weight: both *Camellia Cottage* tea room and *Whelk Coppers* are cosy retreats; *Grey Seal* – a local coffee roaster with several cafés – is the hip newcomer.

From the seafront, the Norfolk Coast Path runs east over grassy Beeston Bump – from where there are good views over the red roofs of Sheringham – then on to the Runtons and Cromer. Going west, the path negotiates the course at Sheringham Golf Club before heading to Cley-next-the-Sea. Another possibility is the Sheringham Circular Walk, six miles into the countryside and back again, all clearly signposted.

Rainy days can be passed in the *Little Theatre* (which also shows films), at *Sheringham Museum* (where there's a modern exhibition on the Sheringham Shoal Offshore Wind Farm) or at the *Fishermen's Heritage Centre*. To fully step back in time, come for the popular 1940s weekend, held in September.

CROMER

Arrive in Cromer on the little Bittern Line train and you'll already be tuned in to the slow pace of this resort. The town was a fashionable spot in the 1800s, and buildings from that era, such as the *Hotel de Paris*, give the seafront a certain sophistication. Times have changed, of course, but Cromer is still a charmer, with a busy, compact centre surrounded by pretty countryside.

The town is protected from the North Sea by a wall of concrete; the effect is softened by the flint cobbles of the wall just behind, but all eyes are usually focused on the splendid pier. It's home to the *Pavilion Theatre* (one of the few still producing variety shows), the offshore lifeboat station and a fireworks display on New Year's Day. The uncluttered promenade has beach huts, a few kiosks and cafés – *North Sea Coffee Co* is one of the few modern examples – and the Glide Surf School. The waves come crashing down here, and surfing takes place winter and summer. The beach is shingle then glorious sand, marshalled by wooden groynes as far as the eye can see. Just along from the pier is a larger patch of shingle with boats and tractors (used to get the boats in and out of the water); nearby is the *RNLI Henry Blogg Museum*. The Norfolk Coast Path runs along the front; follow it to the eastern edge of town, where the huts peter out and the view is of sand, sea and green cliffs into the distance. On the clifftop is North Lodge Park, where there's a small café; a bit further on is the Royal Cromer Golf Club. West of the pier lies East and West Runton, then Sheringham; there are a lot of caravans in between. The Weaver's Way long-distance footpath leads into the countryside; National Trust-owned *Felbrigg Hall* is three miles along the route.

The main town is steps away from the seafront, with small-scale amusements, ice-creams and bucket-and-spade shops to the fore. Independents rule the roost, with the usual mix of gift, junk and charity shops, plus one-offs such as *Harald's* (chocolates and sweets), *Yappers & Barkers* (dog apparel) and *Bookworms* (second-hand books). *Grey Seal*, the local coffee roasters, have an outlet, too. Fish and chips connoisseurs are spoilt for choice: *Mary Jane's* is the homey, traditional option, and *No.1* is the modern alternative, an initiative from nearby gourmet hotel Morston Hall. The famous Cromer crab isn't hard to find either: *Davies* fishmongers sells them dressed, as does *J Lee*, from a stall outside a cottage on New Street.

INDEX

Best For

architecture:
Bexhill 88–9
Brighton 105–6
Eastbourne 94, 95
Felixstowe 21
Folkestone 65–7
Frinton-on-Sea 31
Harwich & Dovercourt 24
Hastings 83
Hove 109–10
Pevensey Bay 92–3
Ramsgate 54
St Leonards-on-Sea 86
Thorpeness 17
Westgate-on-Sea 46

bird-watching:
Canvey Island 40
Dungeness 73
Dunwich 15
Harwich & Dovercourt 24
Holkham 141
Hunstanton 139
Pevensey Bay 92–3
Selsey 125–6
West Wittering 129

boat trips:
Aldeburgh 19
Dover 61
Felixstowe 21
Thorpeness 17
Walton-on-the-Naze 27

cliffs:
Bournemouth 135–6
Broadstairs 51
Cromer 147
Dover 61, 62, 74
Dungeness 74
Dunwich 15
Eastbourne 94, 95
Felixstowe 21
Folkestone 66, 67, 74
Frinton-on-Sea 30–1
Hastings 83, 84, 92
Hunstanton 138–9
Margate 50
Newhaven 100–1, 112
Pevensey Bay 92
Ramsgate 54, 56–7
Rottingdean 103–4
Seaford 99
Shoreham-on-Sea 112
Southend-on Sea 35–6
Walton-on-the-Naze 27
Westgate-on-Sea 46–7
Winchelsea Beach 80

crabbing:
Southwold 10
Walberswick 12

culture:
art
Bexhill 8, 88–9
Bournemouth 136

Brighton 106
Eastbourne 94, 95
Folkestone 7, 65–7
Hastings 7, 83, 84
Hove 109, 110
Margate 7, 49
Rottingdean 103–4
Seaford 99
Southend-on Sea 35–6
St Leonards-on-Sea 86–7
Walton-on-the-Naze 27
Winchelsea Beach 81

cinemas
Aldeburgh 19
Bexhill 88
Broadstairs 52
Camber 7, 77–9
Folkestone 66
Harwich & Dovercourt 23
Hastings 85
St Leonards-on-Sea 87
Westgate-on-Sea 46
Worthing 114

music
Brighton 106
Broadstairs 51–2
Eastbourne 94
Hastings 85
Ramsgate 56
Sandgate 69
Whitstable 41

families:
Camber 77–9
Cromer 146–7
East Beach Littlehampton 116

Eastbourne 94–5
Felixstowe 21
Folkestone 67
Frinton-on-Sea 30–1
Harwich & Dovercourt 24
Hastings 83–5
Holkham 141
Hunstanton 138–9
Margate 49–50
Rottingdean 103
Sheringham 143
Southend-on Sea 35
Southwold 9–10
Thorpeness 17–18
Walton-on-the-Naze 26
Worthing 113–14

festivals:
Aldeburgh 20
Brighton 106
Broadstairs 51
Folkestone 65
Hastings 85
Leigh-on-Sea 39
Sandgate 69
Southend-on Sea 36
Whitstable 42

fish & chips:
Aldeburgh 19
Brighton 105, 106
Clacton-on-Sea 34
Cromer 147
Deal 59
Dungeness 74
Dunwich 15
East Beach Littlehampton 116

fish & chips (*Continued*)
East Wittering 127
Folkestone 66, 67
Frinton-on-Sea 30–1
Harwich & Dovercourt 23
Hastings 85
Herne Bay 44
Holkham 142
Hove 109
Hunstanton 138
Leigh-on-Sea 38
Margate 49
Pevensey Bay 93
Ramsgate 54
Southend-on Sea 35, 36
Southwold 10
Walberswick 13
Walton-on-the-Naze 26
Whitstable 42

food:
Aldeburgh 20
Brighton 106
Broadstairs 52
Camber 78
Deal 60
Folkestone 66, 67
Hastings 84–5
Hove 109
Hythe 71
Leigh-on-Sea 38
Margate 49
Sandgate 68–9
Southwold 10
St Leonards-on-Sea 87
Whitstable 42

history and ancient monuments:
Deal 59–60
Dover 61
Felixstowe 21–2
Harwich & Dovercourt 23
Hastings 83–5
Herne Bay 44–5
Hythe 72–3
Newhaven 100–1
Pevensey Bay 92
Shoreham-on-Sea 111–12
Walton-on-the-Naze 26
Winchelsea Beach 80–1

ice-cream:
Aldeburgh 19
Bexhill 88
Brighton 105
Camber 77
Clacton-on-Sea 33
Cromer 147
East Wittering 127
Eastbourne 94, 95
Frinton-on-Sea 30
Hastings 85
Herne Bay 44
Hove 110
Pevensey Bay 92
Southend-on Sea 36
Southwold 9
Walberswick 12
Worthing 114

nightlife:
Bournemouth 135
Brighton 105, 106
Hastings 85

Hove 110
Margate 49
Southend 35–6

old-fashioned appeal:
Bognor Regis 121–2
Broadstairs 51
Felixstowe 21
Frinton-on-Sea 30–1
Herne Bay 44
Hythe 72
Seaford 99
Sheringham 143
Westgate-on-Sea 46–7
Worthing 114

one-off resorts:
Canvey Island 40
Dungeness 73
Leigh-on-Sea 39
Thorpeness 17
Walberswick 12

piers:
Bognor Regis 121
Bournemouth 135, 136, 137
Brighton 105
Clacton-on-Sea 33
Cromer 146, 147
Deal 59
Eastbourne 94, 95
Felixstowe 21
Harwich & Dovercourt 23
Hastings 83, 85
Herne Bay 44, 45
Southend-on Sea 35

Southwold 9
Walton-on-the-Naze 26
Worthing 113

pubs:
Aldeburgh 19
Brighton 105, 106
Broadstairs 52
Camber 77, 78, 79
Deal 59, 60
Dungeness 74
Eastbourne 95
Harwich & Dovercourt 23
Hastings 84–5
Herne Bay 44
Holkham 142
Hove 109, 110
Hythe 72
Leigh-on-Sea 38
Sandgate 68
Southwold 10
Walberswick 12
Whitstable 41
Winchelsea Beach 81

rainy days:
Bournemouth 135–7
Brighton 106
Camber 78
Eastbourne 94–5
Folkestone 65–7
Hastings 83–5
Hunstanton 138–9
Margate 49–50
Sheringham 144
Southend-on-Sea 35–6
Worthing 113–14

sandy beaches:
Bournemouth 135–7
Broadstairs 51
Camber 77–9
Clacton-on-Sea 33
Frinton-on-Sea 30–1
Harwich & Dovercourt 24
Holkham 141–2
Margate 49–50
Ramsgate 56
West Wittering 129–30
Westgate-on-Sea 46–7

shopping:
Aldeburgh 19
Bexhill 88
Bournemouth 136
Brighton 105, 106
Broadstairs 51, 52
Camber 77, 78
Cromer 147
Deal 59–60
Eastbourne 95
Felixstowe 22
Folkestone 66
Frinton-on-Sea 30
Hastings 84
Herne Bay 45
Holkham 142
Hove 109, 110
Hythe 72
Leigh-on-Sea 39
Margate 49
Ramsgate 54, 56
Sandgate 68
Seaford 99

Sheringham 143
Southend-on Sea 36
Southwold 9
St Leonards-on-Sea 87
Westgate-on-Sea 46
Whitstable 41
Worthing 113–14

vintage shops:
Bexhill 89–90
Bournemouth 136
Brighton 106
Deal 59
Folkestone 66
Hastings 83–5
Hove 109
Ramsgate 56
St Leonards-on-Sea 87
Worthing 113

winter trips:
Broadstairs 51
Camber 77
Canvey Island 40
Deal 59–60
Dungeness 74
Folkestone 65–7
Hastings 83–5
Holkham 141
Margate 49, 50
Southwold 9–10
Thorpeness 17
West Beach Littlehampton
    118, 120
Westgate-on-Sea 46–7
West Wittering 129–30

Thanks to Katy Attfield, Brian Beesley, Howard Binysh, Julie Binysh, Jeremy Brill, Ian Crow, Laura Crow, Jan Fuscoe, Tracey Grant, Kathleen Guy, Susan Guy, Annette Hale, Gary Hale, Julia Hamilton, Ruth Jarvis, Daisy Malivoire, Karen Malivoire, Philip Malivoire, Jane Marshall, May Marshall, Fran Paffard, Juliet Peters, Michael Peters, Cath Phillips, Chris Pierre, Rosamund Sales and Yolanda Zappaterra, who all helped with the book, and to Jennifer Alexander, who suggested Emily Feaver as the illustrator.

1 3 5 7 9 10 8 6 4 2

Ebury Press, an imprint of Ebury Publishing,
20 Vauxhall Bridge Road,
London, SW1V 2SA

Ebury Press is part of the Penguin Random House group of companies
whose addresses can be found at global.penguinrandomhouse.com

Copyright © Sarah Guy 2018
Illustrations © Emily Feaver 2018

Sarah Guy has asserted her right to be identified as the author of this Work in
accordance with the Copyright, Designs and Patents Act 1988

First published by Ebury Press in 2018

www.penguin.co.uk

A CIP catalogue record for this book is available from the British Library

ISBN 9781785038631

Typeset in 10.5/14 pt Garamond MT Std
by Integra Software Services Pvt. Ltd, Pondicherry

Printed and bound in Great Britain by Clays Ltd, St Ives PLC

Penguin Random House is committed to a sustainable future for
our business, our readers and our planet. This book is made from
Forest Stewardship Council® certified paper.